Shrub End

**Published by
David Cleveland
2023**

Front cover picture: All Saints, Shrub End. pre1906
Cover Design: Adam Rickwood

Shrub End

Ken Rickwood

Published by
David Cleveland
Manningtree, Essex

ISBN   978-1-9993672-8-2

First published October 2023

British Library Cataloguing-in-Publication Data
A catalogue record for this book is available from
The British Library

Designed by
Ken Rickwood

Printed in England by
Lavenham Press Ltd

Also by
Ken Rickwood
Lighting up Colchester 2001
Stour Secrets 2008
Stour Odyssey 2010
The Colne 2013
Colchester's Secret Roman River 2019
Blackwater 2021

available from localeastanglianbooks.com

CONTENTS

ACKNOWLEDGEMENTS

This book would not have been possible without the help of many people, past and present. I have consulted many books and those listed in the bibliography have all provided me with useful information, but many more have provided an odd snippet here and there. I am indebted to the many individuals who have helped me and I hope that if I fail to mention a name, where I should, it will be forgiven.

I have tried to ascertain the copyright of all the pictures that I have used and included an attribution where appropriate, those unattributed are either in my own collection or photographs I have taken during my wanderings researching this book.

Individuals and organisations whose help I would like to acknowledge are; Roger Allen, Alan & Wendy Baird, Leona Bryan, Lindi Burroughs, David Cleveland, Colchester Library, Christina Edwards, Andrew English, Essex Record Office, Daphne Jones, Chris & Melvyn Joscelyne, Lexden History Group, David & Jennifer Millin, Bernard Polley, John Sanders, Liz White.

Extracts from Ordnance Survey maps are reproduced with the kind permission of Ordnance Survey.

INTRODUCTION

I have to thank Ben Robinson for the inspiration to write this account of the village in which I have lived for over fifty years. I had forgotten that when I first moved here many of my neighbours referred to the area as 'the village'. It was after reading Ben's book, *England's Villages* I realized that although where I live is now within the bounds of the city of Colchester there survive many features of the village of Shrub End in which my house was built in 1929. This book is an account of what I know of the village and parish of Shrub End.

The first question is, where exactly is Shrub End? Various individuals and authorities have provided me with different answers. For the purposes of the history of the village I have chosen the ecclesiastical parish of Shrub End. This is centered on the church of All Saints. The boundaries of this relatively new parish have changed little during its short life. The ecclesiastical parish includes only a part of the District Council Ward of Shrub End along with a significant part of Prettygate Ward and some of Stanway Ward. When it comes to the ever-changing Parliamentary Constituency areas, parts of the parish are within Colchester, some in Witham with others that may shortly end up in Harwich and North Essex.

Historically the boundaries of the area known as Shrub End have always been difficult to define. Early references do not specify exactly where it was other than being somewhere on the ancient road between Colchester and Maldon. By early Victorian times it had come to mean all those farms and habitations along the stretch of this road where it formed the boundary between the established parishes of Lexden and Stanway. Quite how far Shrub End extended into these parishes on either side of the road seemed to be somewhat arbitrary.

Then in 1845 the redundant church of All Saints Stanway, which is now in ruins in the grounds of Colchester Zoo, was replaced by a new church built at Bottle End. Parts of the north-east of ancient Stanway along with parts of Lexden were transferred into the new parish. During the following hundred years or so the population of the area grew and developed its own identity. As a result in 1960 the name of the church and parish, with minor boundary alterations was changed from All Saints' Stanway to All Saints' Shrub End.

Then for the first time the boundaries of Shrub End were officially defined. This book is about its 1200 acres (480 ha) and those people who have lived and worked on them over the centuries.

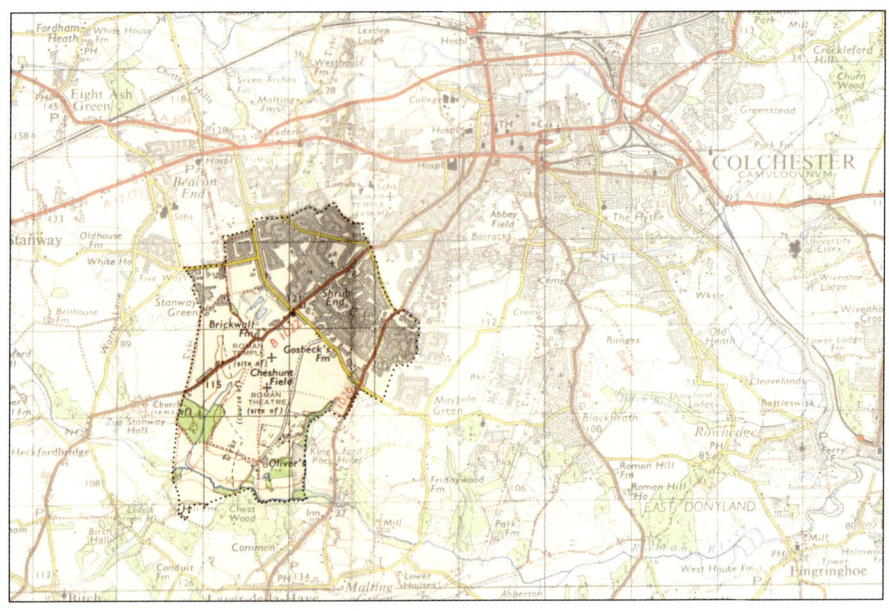

The parish of Shrub End lies south-west of Colchester City centre.

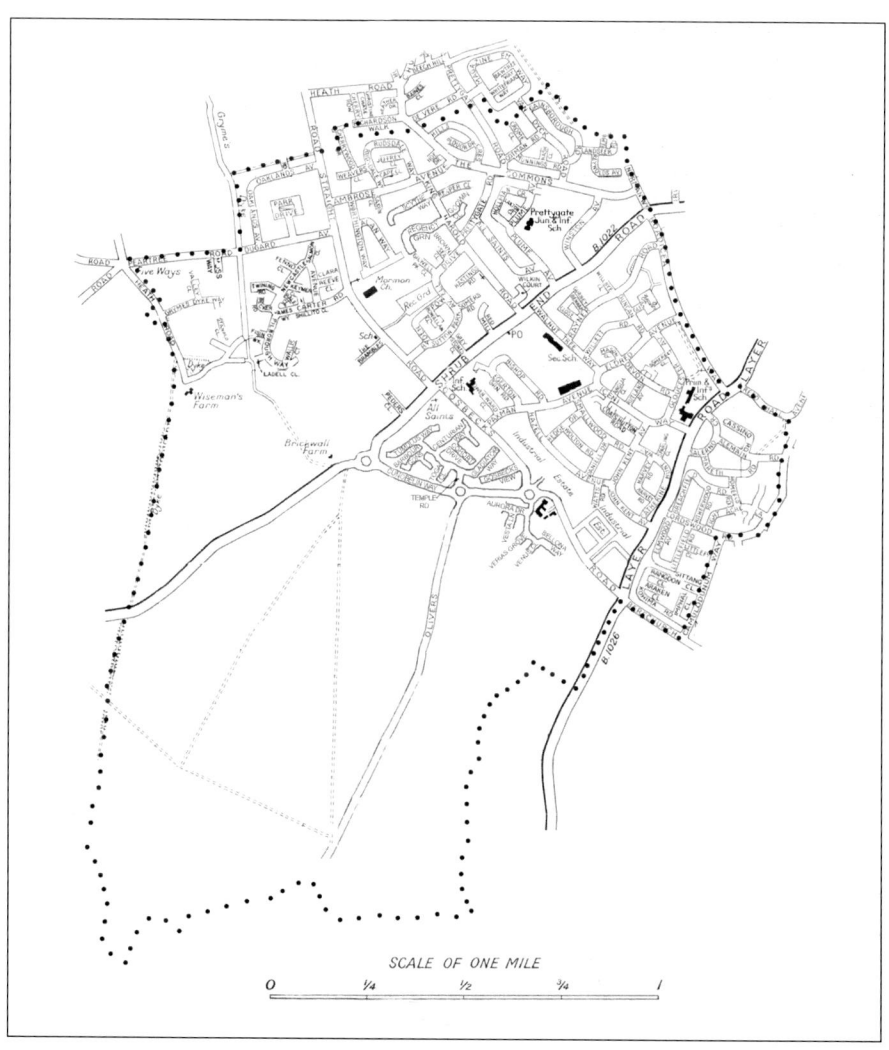

The ecclesiastical parish of Shrub End includes the Shrub End Estate, substantial parts of Prettygate, Colchester Archaeological Park, some ex-MOD land, and Stanway Green.

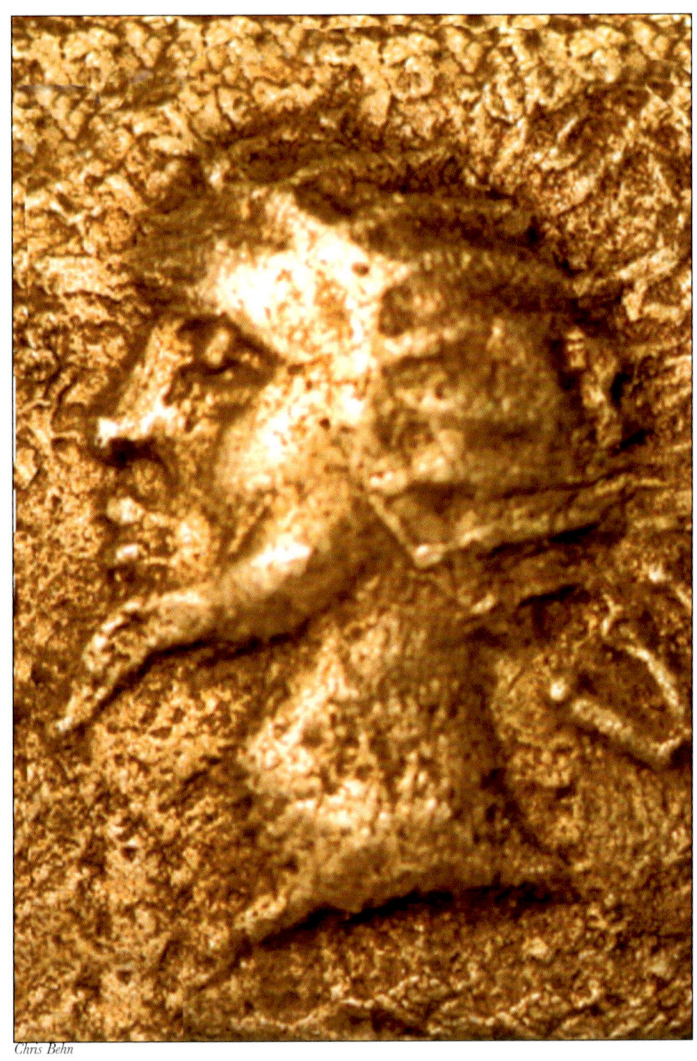

An image of Cunobelin, King of the Britons, taken from one of the many coins minted in Camulodunum bearing his name.

CHAPTER 1

Home of Kings and Buried Treasure

I have found this to be a good place to live. It always has been and was recognized as such as soon as the Ancient Britons abandoned the hunter-gatherer way of life for that of settlement and farming. Little is known of the earliest Britons who settled here but by the time of the late Iron Age, 200BCE-43CE large areas of southern Britain were relatively densely populated and organised into tribes. There was often rivalry between these Celtic tribes who were also aware of the expanding influence of the Roman Empire across the channel and one of the British tribal leaders sought help from Rome to settle a dispute.

This gave Julius Caesar the excuse to cross the channel in 55BCE. A combination of bad weather and a hostile reception by the natives forced him to abandon the venture but he returned the following year with a better-equipped navy and a larger army. This time Caesar succeeded in making contact with several tribal leaders including the one who had sought his assistance.

Not only did this venture lead to the establishment of closer trading links with Rome it also left us with Caesar's account of what he had seen and learnt about the Britons, their methods of war, their expert horsemanship, and the thousands of chariots they could deploy in inter-tribal conflict. This is the earliest written record of Britain and its inhabitants.

Despite nearly a hundred years of increasing trade and friendly relations between Rome and the tribes of south-east Britain, in 43CE the Roman emperor Claudius launched an invasion. Eventually he reached the headquarters of the most powerful of the British tribal leaders, Cunobelin, who was a descendant of the leader who had sought Caesar's help all those years earlier.

Cunobelin's tribal base was an area of relatively flat, fertile land situated between the River Colne and Roman River extending out as far as Stanway. This triangular area of some ten square miles was protected on two sides by rivers and on the third by a series of dykes. These were not all built at the same time but each was a substantial structure several miles long. It must have required the organization and deployment of many men to shift the thousands of tons of earth to build them.

The surviving stretches of these dykes remain impressive some 2000 years later. Archaeological investigation shows that when first constructed each consisted of a rampart about 10ft (3m) in height with a ditch of a similar depth alongside. Some of the ramparts would have been surmounted by a timber palisade. With or without a palisade these dykes would have created a formidable barrier to infantry, cavalry and charioteers.

The whole of Shrub End lies within Cunobelin's fortified area of Camulodunum and his personal stronghold at Gosbecks was located in the modern parish. Archaeological investigations and crop marks have revealed that this exceptionally large farmstead within its own ditched enclosure was surrounded by fields and pasture with interconnecting droveways. Nearby there would have been sacred areas at springs and in isolated wooded groves. This was the centre of power administered by Cunobelin, leader of the Trinovantes, the most powerful of the British Celtic tribes.

The earliest defences for Camulodunum.
1 – Heath Farm dyke. 2 – Lexden/ Moat farm dyke. 3 – Sheepen dyke.

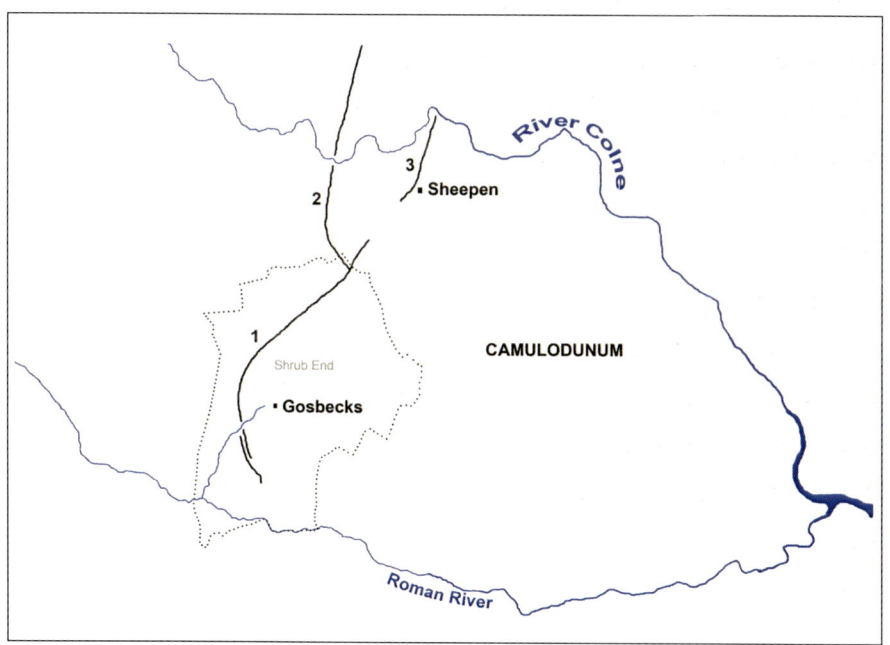

Throughout the vast defended area of Camulodunum there would have been numerous farmsteads, homesteads, and workshops, each lived in by individuals bound by kinship or interest. All traces of many of these have completely disappeared but one significant area, which was first excavated during the 1930s, has yielded much information about the manufacturing and commercial activities of the Trinovantes. This was on the banks of the River Colne at Sheepen. Here the remains of ovens, hearths, crucibles, tools, and scrap provide evidence of pre-Roman metal working in copper, bronze, iron, silver, and gold, the latter being cast and minted into coins. It is estimated that over a million gold coins were struck bearing the name Cunobelin.

A gold coin struck at the Sheepen mint bearing an image of Cunobelin, referred to by some as the King of the Britons.

Chris Behn

A gold coin struck at the Sheepen mint bearing an image of an ear of corn representing the agricultural fertility of the area and CAMU for Camulodunum. The reverse carries an image of a horse, a symbol of power and the letters CUNO for Cunobelin.

Chris Behn

The route taken by the Celts between Cunobelin's power centre at Gosbecks and his mint and manufacturing centre at Sheepen must have passed through Shrub End. Some traces of this route may survive in dykes, field boundaries, footpaths and roads.

Much superficial evidence has been obliterated by the developments made over the last hundred years or so but the basic landform remains the same. This and the earliest OS maps are helpful in determining the possible route taken by the earliest inhabitants of Shrub End between Gosbecks and Sheepen.

Back at Gosbecks and the dramatic arrival of Claudius. No doubt his army had to fight to get there, but what happened then is far from clear. Tribes that submitted by diplomacy were given some independence in return for loyalty to Rome. Submission is far more likely than conflict as Claudius began his return to Rome a few days after arriving at the stronghold of the Trinovantes, triumphant and claiming the submission of many British tribes. Most of the invading army moved on but the Twentieth Legion (XX) stayed and built a legionary fortress within Trinovante territory but it was on unoccupied high ground. This became the western half of the present walled town of Colchester. When the legion moved out, to quell a rebellion elsewhere, what they had built was expanded into a colonia, a self-governing extension of Rome. This was peopled by retired soldiers who to honour their service had been given Roman citizenship.

It is difficult to know how the two communities interacted. History tends to record the dramatic events and is invariably written by the victorious whereas archaeology often reveals a more subtle story. One of Cunobelin's descendants, Caratacus, was definitely not for living under Roman domination. He moved west with his wealth and followers to remain a thorn in the side of the Romans until his eventual defeat in battle. He was taken to Rome where he was paraded in chains and humiliated as a criminal.

Of those who remained at Gosbecks some may have been more enthusiastic to embrace the Roman way of life, but not all. Within a few years Boudica arrived with her followers who totally destroyed the colonia built by the Romans. No doubt she was joined by many Trinovantes on her march onto London, St Albans and the rest.

Eventually the Romans regained control and rebuilt their colonia on the hill. But this time it was heavily defended by a substantial wall, parts of which survive today. Within a generation it appears past hostilities were put aside and the Gosbecks site continued to flourish with the native inhabitants adopting many aspects of Roman culture.

Archaeological evidence reveals that an impressive theatre and temple complex were built on the Gosbecks site around 100 CE. The site was discovered in 1842 by Rev Henry Jenkins during the earliest archaeological excavation in Colchester. But the function of the site was not determined until further investigations had been carried out by several archaeologists and by 1967 its religious use had been established and an earlier wooden structure had been discovered below the Roman theatre site. The temple is now described by archaeologists as Romano-Celtic because it represents a fusion of the religious beliefs of both Romans and Celts.

The dedication of the temple is unknown but the discovery in 1939 of a fine bronze statue of Mercury nearby suggests that he could have been the focus of worship. Mercury was god of many things but perhaps most relevant to Gosbecks, the fleet-footed messenger of the gods was the god of abundance and commercial success. It is thought that large numbers of visitors could have come to Gosbecks for a variety of festivals and religious ceremonies. These activities would have taken place in the open air at both the theatre and temple.

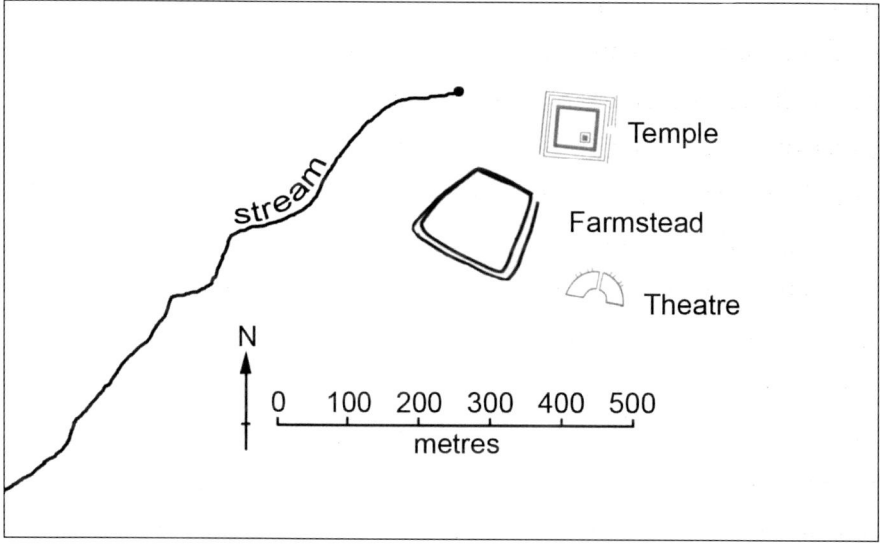

The close proximity of the pre-Roman and Roman buildings indicate that this was an important administrative, commercial and religious site both before and after the arrival of the Romans.

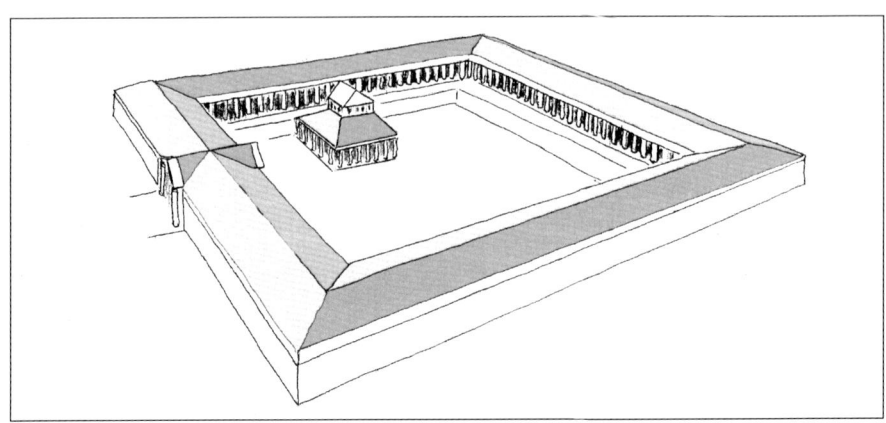

An impression of how the Romano-Celtic temple could have been. It comprised an outer building, a portico, which was a covered walkway around all four sides of the temple complex and was open on the inside. This allowed visitors to walk or stand in the portico and view the ceremonies taking place in the inner temple area.

An impression of how the Roman theatre may have been.

The building of such a large Romano-Celtic complex on the site of earlier religious significance shows there must have been a significant population happy to take advantage of the benefits the Roman way of life brought to their lives.

The whole of south-east England is dotted with the sites of Roman villas. In Essex alone there are over 60 known villa sites. Those closest to Colchester include those at Great Tey, Fordham, Stanway, Layer Breton, Abberton, Alresford, Brightlingsea, St Osyth, and several on Mersea Island but there were none within the Gosbecks area. Some farmsteads had the characteristics of grander villas albeit on a less impressive scale. An example of one such home was discovered within the Gosbecks area in 1994. This was on the Kirkee McMunn barracks site when a simple Roman farmstead of moderate status was revealed by an archaeological investigation.

The inhabitants of other colonia established in Britain were allocated land in the surrounding area to farm for the support of their community. This was often laid out in a series of regular rectangular plots, a Roman method of establishing field boundaries called centuriation. This appears not to have happened to any great extent around Colchester, maybe out of respect for the local inhabitants or because as at Gosbecks there was a pre-existing network of farmsteads, fields and trackways which the locals were prepared to work for their new masters. The only significant exception to this revealed to date is at the farmstead discovered at the Kirkee McMunn barracks site, which was associated with the presence of some field patterns, which could have been centuriation. Although this lies within Cunobelin's fortified area of Camulodunum it is at its eastern extremity, far from the religious centre.

Several generations lived their increasingly Romanised lives peacefully, but no community is immune to outside influences. By the late 200s CE instability in Gaul and incursions by northern Europeans led to a period of instability in Britain. At Gosbecks the theatre and temple were abandoned and the people fled, possibly to the abandoned colonia as a place offering more security against incoming marauders. At least one of those who left the Gosbecks site at this time was wealthy. They buried their silver coins in pots and failed to return to recover them. The pots laid undisturbed until 1983 when Brian Wade was ploughing at Oliver's Orchard and noticed some coins glistening in the plough soil. He gathered up the handful of coins and took them to the Orchards owner, Rupert Knowles, who notified Colchester Museum of the find. A team of Museum staff and volunteers from Colchester Archaeological Group searched the area and recovered four pots and over 6000 coins. The site of this find was about 400m from the theatre and temple complex.

It is not known if the Gosbecks site was populated during the turbulent times of the decline of Roman rule and the ascent of Saxon domination. And if it was, was it by the indigenous Romanised Celts or the incoming Saxons? It is claimed by historians that the Romans left Britain in 410 CE because their homes in Italy were being attacked by fierce tribes and every soldier was needed back in Rome. In fact the decline of Roman authority and control in Britain was patchy and gradual. The first Saxons to appear in the area could well have been mercenaries working for the Romans and seeing their decline of authority encouraged their friends and family to join them. This could have been a relatively swift and peaceful take over. On the other hand the complete failure of Roman administration could have left large areas of the country in a state of anarchy and several years of uncertainty.

From historical records it is known that Colchester was a Roman town until at least 409 CE and the earliest archaeological evidence of Saxon occupation is around 440-450 CE. These dates relate to what was going on within the walls; it is not known how this affected the surrounding hinterland. Further archaeological investigation on the Gosbecks site could shed more light on any possible early Saxon occupation.

An Anglo-Saxon coin bearing the name Sigered,
the last King of Essex.

CHAPTER 2

Saxons and the Manor of Shrebbe

From the scant evidence uncovered to date it appears the change from Roman to Saxon domination was less of an invasion and more of a period of relatively peaceful coexistence with the indigenous population. With the Saxon settlers in the minority the Romano-British landscape very probably remained largely unchanged. That is not to say there were not conflicts between rival incoming groups. But no evidence has come to light of any of these happening within the area that became Shrub End.

After a century or so the kingdom of Essex emerged by the amalgamation of smaller subkingdoms and Saxon tribal groups. The Saxon Kings of Essex issued coins of a similar pattern to those issued by Cunobelin simultaneously asserting a link to the 1st century rulers while emphasising their independence.

Eventually Sigered, the last king of an independent Essex, ceded power, leading to Essex becoming a shire within the kingdom of Edward the Elder, son of Alfred the Great and King of all Anglo-Saxons. From then on the King's representative in Essex was styled an Earldorman.

The Saxon method of government was less hierarchical than the Roman system with considerable control devolved to local leaders. Each of these controlled an area that varied between a few acres and a few hundred acres, and was called a manor and the person in charge was the lord of the manor. The lord administered the manor and was responsible for justice, security and the wellbeing of those within his manor. All those who lived there were allocated some land that had to be worked. The serfs worked their own land and also that of the lord; the freemen worked their own land and paid the lord a fee in lieu of labour.

The first reasonably complete record of the manors and their lords was made by William the Conqueror in his Domesday survey of 1086. This records 13,418 manors and their owners. By this time the manor of Stanway was recorded as including an area called Lexden and belonged to the King. During Saxon times Stanway had passed to the wife of the Earldorman, Byrthnoth, upon his death at the Battle of Maldon. She willed it to King Harold, hence to King William after the Conquest.

Manor boundaries did not always coincide with Parish boundaries and both have moved about over time. There are records indicating that at various times Stanway has been home of up to ten manors; Abbott's, Belhous or Belhows, Byreton or Barton, Gosbecks, Howes, Kirton, Lexden, Olivers, Stanway, and Shrebb.

The Earldorman, Byrthnoth, who died at the Battle of Maldon in 991.

Shrebb is not recorded in the Domesday survey but that does not mean it did not exist. One of the earliest records of Shrebb dates from 1285 when the Colchester burgesses claimed 16d (6½p) shrebgavel. The element 'gavel' was an ancient term for land tenure based on payment of a rent to a lord instead of labour. Its use suggests that the shrebgavel was a pre-Conquest rent.

In 1276 Shrebb was treated as a separate vill by the forest justices. A vill was the smallest administrative unit under the feudal system, consisting of a number of houses and their adjacent lands, roughly corresponding to the modern parish. In the late 14th century some land and a house in Shreb or Shrub Street paid Colchester borough shrebgavel totalling 11s 11d. (60p).

Henry VII, the first Tudor King, reigned from 1485 to 1509. During this time he gathered huge wealth for the Crown. Among his various acquisitions was the manor of 'Shrebbe in Stanwey'. This may well have been the vill referred to in earlier records.

At the time of these early records there was no standard spelling and scribes wrote down what they heard or copied from other documents resulting in considerable variation.

These few records imply the manor of Shrebb could have existed for at least 500 years, after which it appears to have been broken up and subsumed into adjoining parishes.

1272 Screb, Scrobbe

1276 Shrobben, S(c)hrebbefeld, S(c)hrebbestret,
      S(c)hrebbestrate, S(c)hrebbehows

1291 Scrobbe, Shrobbe

1308 Scebbe(street)

1323 Shribbe

1350 S(c)hrubbe

1500 Shrybbe

c1500 Shrebb

Not every manor had a manor house and some had a building of modest construction. If there was a manor house in Shrebb it is most likely to have been a single storey structure built from timber, infilled with wattle and daub under a thatched roof. There may have been a raised dias, an earthen floor and probably no chimney. Cooking would have been done in a separate building so the hall would not have burnt down in the event of a kitchen fire.

During this period the villagers, peasants, would have lived in single storey long houses. These were single room dwellings in which the villager not only worked, ate and slept but also kept his livestock. These buildings were built without foundations and were intended to last for only twenty to thirty years. It is unlikely that they would leave any evidence of their existence.

It is impossible to know how many people lived in Shrebb but if its population followed the ups and downs of national trends it would have varied considerably. During the early 14th century there was a dramatic climatic downturn, often referred to as the Little Ice Age, which was to last into the 17th century. The ice cold winters and wet summers, resulted in poor harvests and widespread famine. The weakened population was then hit by the bubonic plague, which arrived in England in 1348. If small black buboes appeared on your body it meant you might have only days to live. Hence the common name for this first outbreak was the Black Death. Waves of the plague continued for three centuries claiming the lives of about a third of the population.

The most notable effect of the Black Death was the change in social structure due to the scarcity of labour. There simply were not the numbers of people to work the land. This could well have been a contributory cause of the disappearance of the manor of Shrebb.

In 1768 Philip Morant in his *History and Antiquities of the County of Essex* describes the manor of Shrebb as containing 180 acres (72 ha) lying in the south-east of the parish of Stanway; and partly in the parishes of Lexden and St Mary's at the Walls, Colchester. In 1495 it was held by John Doreward Esq. By the time Philip Morant was writing he stated 'Shrebb was no longer looked upon as a manor, and had no signs of it.'

CHAPTER 3

Farms, Farm Owners and Farmers

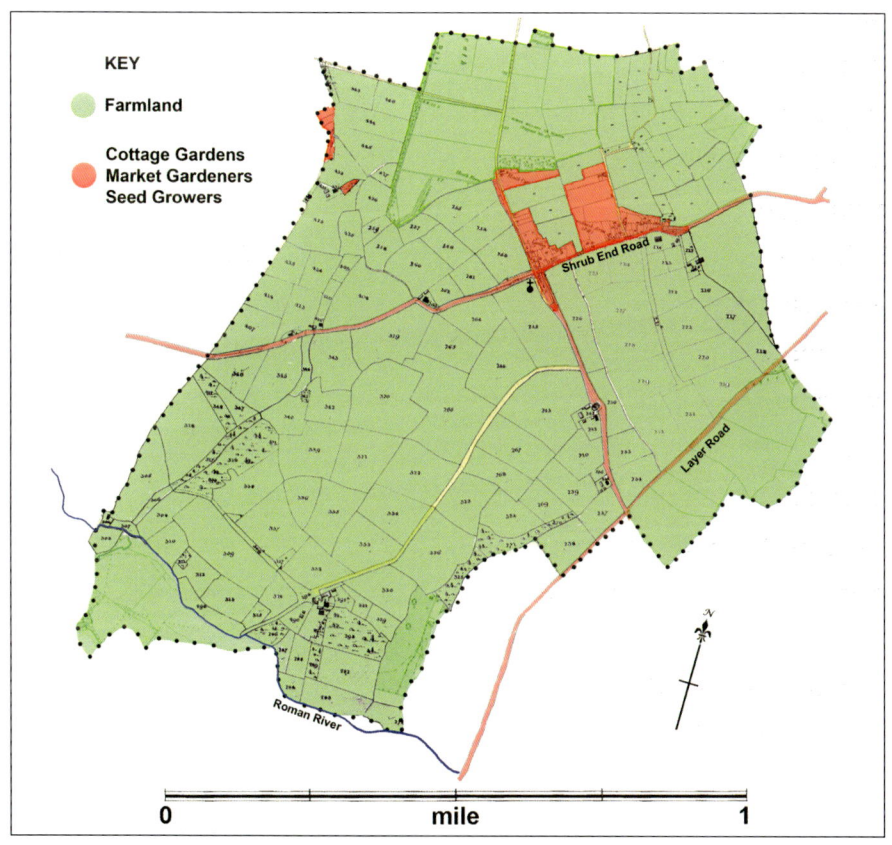

The parish of Shrub End land use in c1840.

For many centuries the life and economy of Shrub End was dominated by farming. Each age had its own somewhat inflexible social structures, which all depended upon the availability of a plentiful supply of labour. The Black Death changed all that. Some villagers who had survived the ravages of the plague realized there was now more land to cultivate than there were people to maintain it; at last they were in a position to better their lot. The large open fields in which each villager looked after his own strip no longer functioned because untended strips grew weeds, which seeded onto adjoining cultivated ones, which made the whole system inefficient and unviable. If the lord of the manor decided it was better to lease or even sell all or some of his land, ambitious villagers could acquire land and rise to join a new social rank, that of the yeoman farmer.

These changes in land ownership began to change the appearance of the countryside as fields began to be enclosed with hedges and fences to demark ownership. Many of the old common fields and wastes became enclosed and the yeomen farmers found they could consolidate their holdings by exchanging distant holdings for ones closer to their homes. Some of the boundaries of these early enclosures followed those of the open fields that were often gentle curves. Remnants of many of these can still be recognized today.

As the population recovered, more land was needed to grow sufficient food. This state of affairs led to much of the remaining common land and open space being enclosed. This time enclosure was not led by

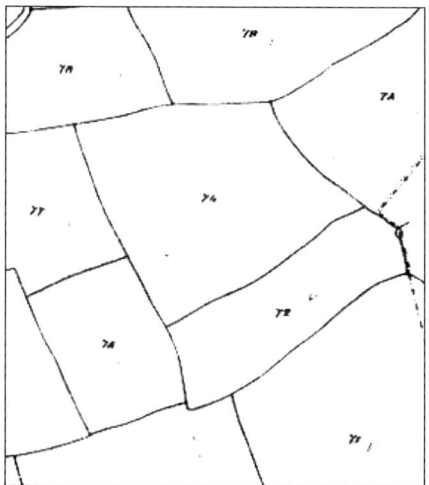 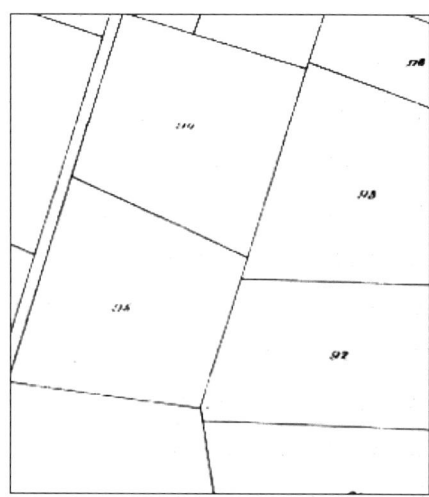

An extract from the Lexden tithe map of 1838 showing curved field boundaries near Plume farm. These could be remnants of the open fields of the manor of Shrebbe.

An extract from the Lexden tithe map of 1838 showing straight field boundaries created after the enclosure of Lexden Heath and Stanway Heath.

the people but forced upon them by those who could afford to enclose land. Many villagers lost their grazing and foraging rights and once more were at the behest of the landowners. Fields created during this period were often rectangular with straight boundaries.

The patterns of land ownership and methods of farming have changed over the centuries but field boundaries, both ancient and those more recently created, tend to remain constant. During the 10th century the Saxon kings wrote into law the tithes act. This required a contribution of 10% of all villager's produce be given to the church. As the patterns of land ownership changed the tithe each landowner paid depended upon the area of land owned. These areas were measured with great precision and once measured it was administratively easier to carry them over from one year to the next. This could be checked easily by an inspection of the field boundaries without labourious re-measurement.

When the new parish of Shrub End was created in 1845 it was still an agricultural community almost entirely dependent on providing for its needs on what could be produced from the parish lands.

A study of farm records, tithe records, census returns, and contemporary maps has made it possible to create a picture of the rural parish of Shrub End before it fell under the influence of the urban tentacles of neighbouring Colchester.

I have based my description of the Shrub End farmlands as they were in the 1830s when recorded on the tithe maps and allocations made at that time. Each field or plot was given a number and its area agreed with the owner or occupier. Each area was recorded in three columns of acres, roods, perches. An acre (0.4 ha) is 4000 square metres; an acre is equal to four rood, ie. ¼ acre or 1000 square metres; and a perch is a 1/40 of a rood, ie. 25 square metres.

1 perch	25 square metres
1 rood	1000 square metres
1 acre	4000 square metres

Much of the history of the comparatively new ecclesiastical parish of Shrub End is contained within the records of the older parishes of Lexden and Stanway. A study of these reveals much information concerning the farmsteads and dwellings along the common boundary between the two parishes, which became Shrub End.

Over time the names of the farms and their boundaries have changed many times. A few have survived to the present day, some have all but disappeared and others exist only in the name of a street or single dwelling.

I have used the relevant areas of tithe maps from the 1840s to determine which farms to write about. Most farms were entirely within the parish but some had land outside the parish and others were situated outside the parish but farmed land within it.

Those along Shrub End Road and Maldon Road were; Plume Farm, Walnut Tree Farm, Rayner's Farm, Brickwall Farm, Well House Farm, and Stanway Hall Farm. Those located further into Stanway were; Gosbecks Farm, Lambert's Farm, New House Farm, Oliver's Farm, and Wiseman's Farm. Those located further into Lexden were; Prettygate Farm, Magazine Farm, and Squirrels Farm. For ease of reference I have written about each in alphabetical order.

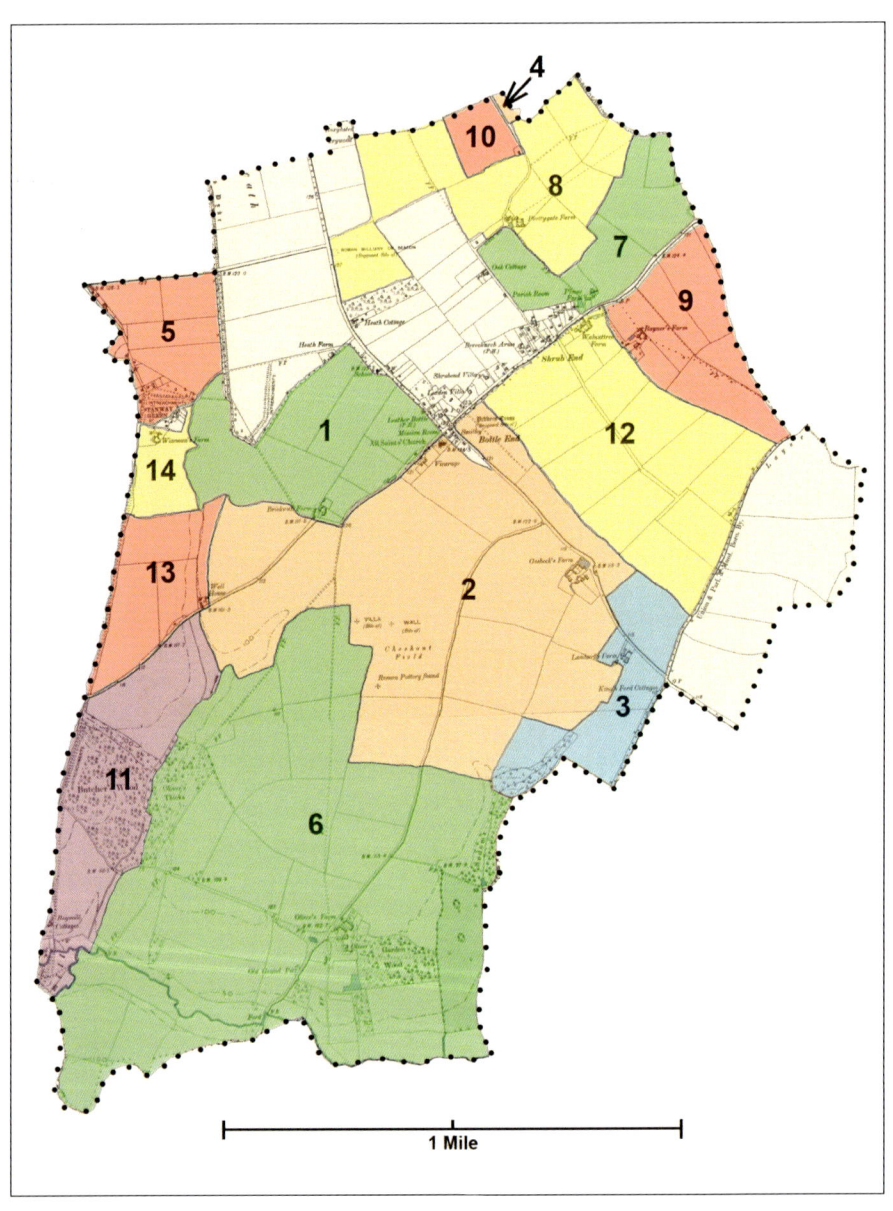

1 Mile

Map of Shrub End parish with the areas of each of the farms coloured and numbered as they existed c1830.

1	Brickwall Farm
2	Gosbecks Farm
3	Lambert's Farm
4	Magazine Farm
5	New House Farm
6	Oliver's Farm
7	Plume Farm
8	Prettygate Farm
9	Rayner's Farm
10	Squirrels Farm
11	Stanway Hall Farm
12	Walnut Tree Farm
13	Well House Farm
14	Wiseman's Farm

1 Brickwall Farm

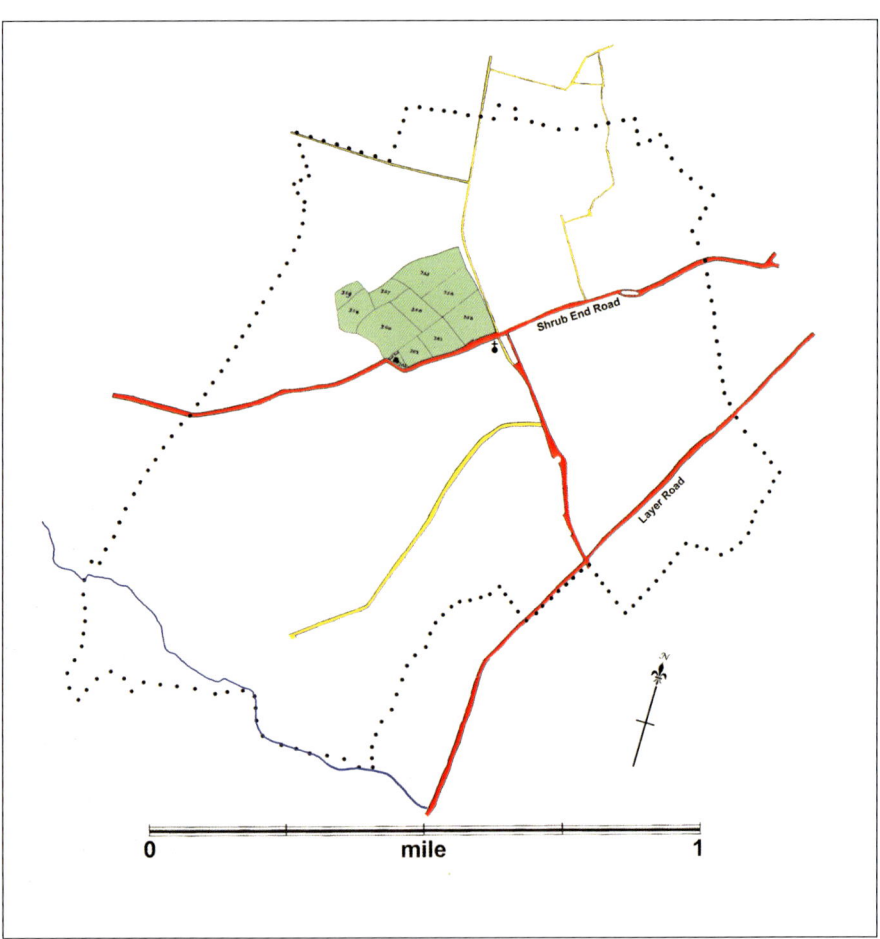

The tithe map of 1839 lists ten fields totalling 63 acres belonging to Brickwall Farm, which at the time was owned and farmed by William Woodward.

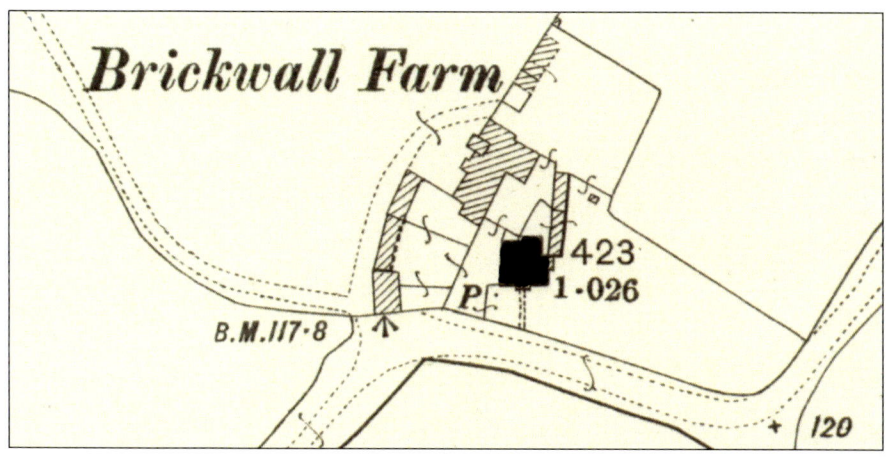

Brickwall Farm buildings
(Farmhouse is black, P is for pump, BM is Bench Mark - height above sea level in feet)

Brickwall Farmhouse is situated on the north side of Shrub End Road opposite the car park of Colchester Archaeological Park. For many years its roadside boundary was the long curved brickwall from which it takes its name. Road alterations made in the 1970s have left it further back but the course of the old road can still be seen as the access to the farm and the track that follows the course of an ancient dyke towards Stanway Green.

The listed building exhibits many 18th century features but they probably cover an older timber-framed structure dating back to Elizabethan times. At that time it was a Stanway Manor property and referred to as Parkefield, a name that it kept into the 19th century. This could have been because it laid on the edge of the extensive park that at one time surrounded a grand Stanway Hall, now in the grounds of Colchester Zoo.

27

The earliest record of the property being referred to as Brick Wall Farm dates from 1758. By 1817 the owner and occupier was listed as William Woodward who also held the lease of Stanway Hall. The Woodward family were to hold several properties in the area during the following century.

For most of its existence the farm's lands amounted to 60-70 acres (24-28ha). Then during the 20th century many were sold off for other uses. For some years now the farmhouse and a couple of the remaining fields, Home Field and part of Barn Field, have been owned by J D Robinson who have an engineering and vehicle hire business in Colchester.

The Brickwall Farm nameplate displayed on the brickwall from which the farm takes its name. 2022

Brickwall Farmhouse. 1936

Christina Edwards

*The timber-framed
Elizabethan Brickwall
Farmhouse behind its
brickwall. Originally this
was lower and before the
road alterations of the 1970s
bordered the road as it swept
around it.*

29

2 Gosbecks Farm

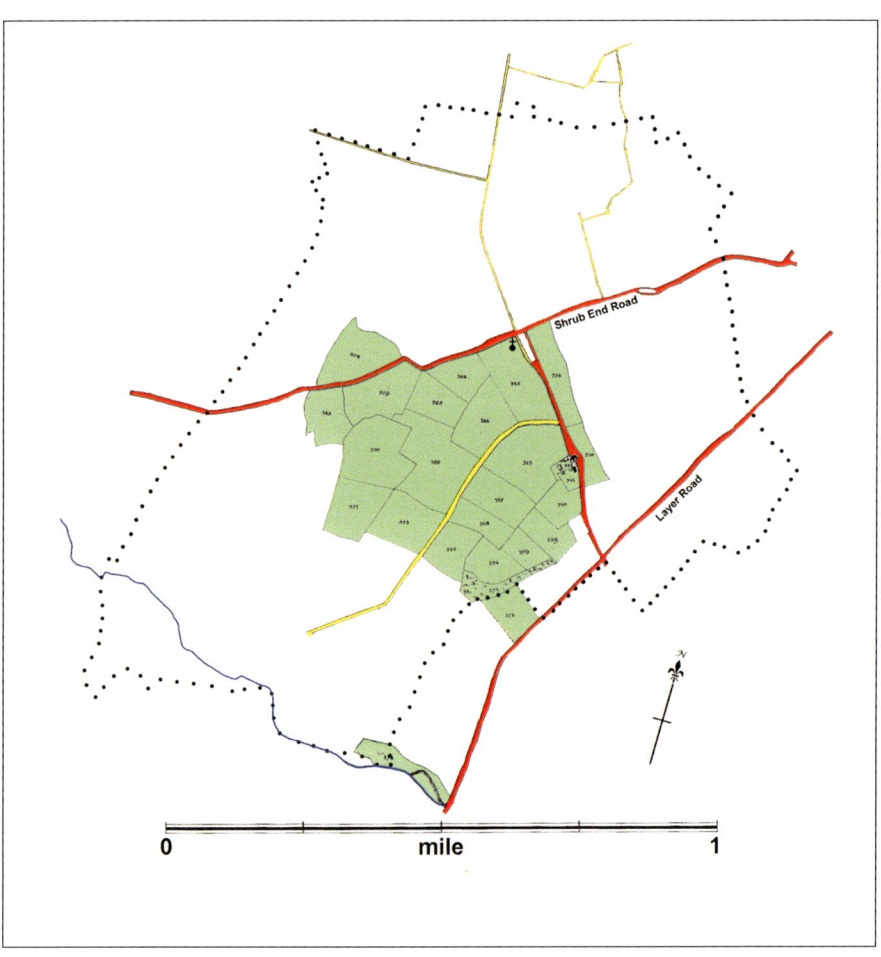

The tithe map of 1839 lists 22 fields totalling 277 acres belonging the farm which at the time was owned Nicholas Tomlinson and farmed by John Root.

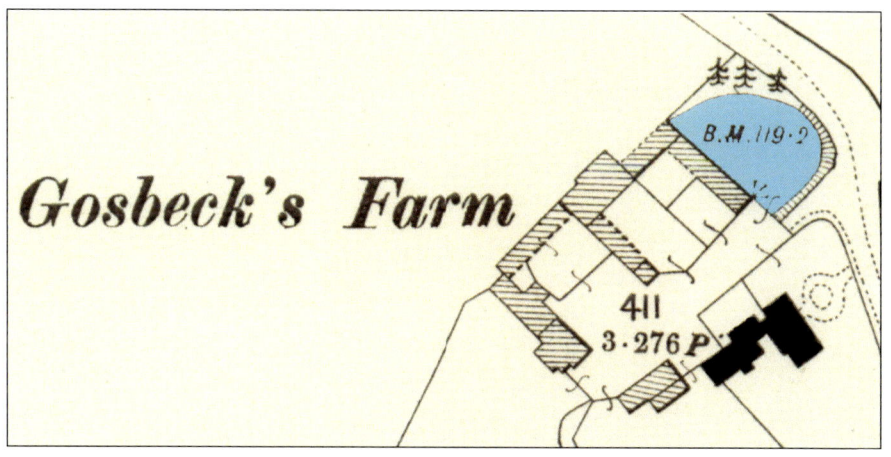

Gosbecks Farm buildings
(Farmhouse is black, pond is blue, P is for pump)

The name, Gosbecks is thought to be associated with the families of Roger de Gosebek (1254) who probably came from Gosbeck in Suffolk. Early documents present a variety of spellings including Gospecks, Gosbacks, and Grassbacks. At one time Gosbecks was a manor in its own right and was held by St John's Abbey, then King Henry VIII, followed by his Chancellor, Thomas Lord Audley, whose descendant, Besney Barker, owned it during the early 1700s. At that time the tenant was James Hellen whose descendants went on to farm at several other places in the area. By 1747 James Hellen had moved on and the new tenant was James Porter who was also the tenant of the adjoining Lambert's farm. During the period of his tenancy the farm was sometimes still referred to as the Manor Farm.

The farmhouse stands on the site of a much earlier building. The front part of the present two-storey building dates from the late 18th century and is of redbrick with a painted front. To the rear is an older timber-framed structure with a tiled hipped roof.

The farm ownership changed several times and was occupied by various tenants until the Barbour family arrived in 1935. This family, like many farming families in Essex, originated in Scotland, came to Gosbecks for its modern cowshed and large area of permanent pasture. The Barbour's dairy herd was expanded and the light soil was improved to grow arable crops. The Barbours were enthusiastic mechanics and engineers who enjoyed experimenting with and adapting farm machinery. It was not surprising that in 1936 Gosbecks saw the first combine harvester in Essex, an experimental prototype. Farmers came from far and wide to scoff at the idea saying 'it would never catch on and replace the reliable old binder'.

Bernard Polley

The first combine harvester in Essex,
an experimental prototype being used at Gosbecks Farm. 1936

WWII brought many changes to the farm. As part of the Government's efforts to increase food production some pasture was ploughed and 'land girls' and German POWs from the nearby Berechurch Camp were employed. Also part of the farm pasture area was used as an airstrip for glider pilot training.

Post war, the farm returned to normal for a few years but the economic situation had changed in favour of specialisation and it became clear the days of mixed farming were over. The dairy herd was sold, the pasture ploughed and potatoes became the main crop.

33

Bernard Polley

Gosbecks pond. 1950s

The site of the former Gosbecks pond. 2022

These required irrigation and fertiliser, unsurprisingly this method of farming, too, soon became uneconomic. The Barbours continued interest in engineering led them to host the East Anglian Traction Engine Club's Sixth Annual Rally in 1960.

By 1985 David Barbour, the third generation of Barbours to farm Gosbecks decided that the farm needed a new direction and proposed the creation of an Archaeological Park. Over ten years later after long negotiation with Colchester Borough Council the park was officially opened in 1998.

Since then further small areas of the farmland have been used for residential development but the majority has remained as open grassland.

Traction Engine Rally held at Gosbecks farm. 1960

Bernard Polley

3 Lambert's Farm

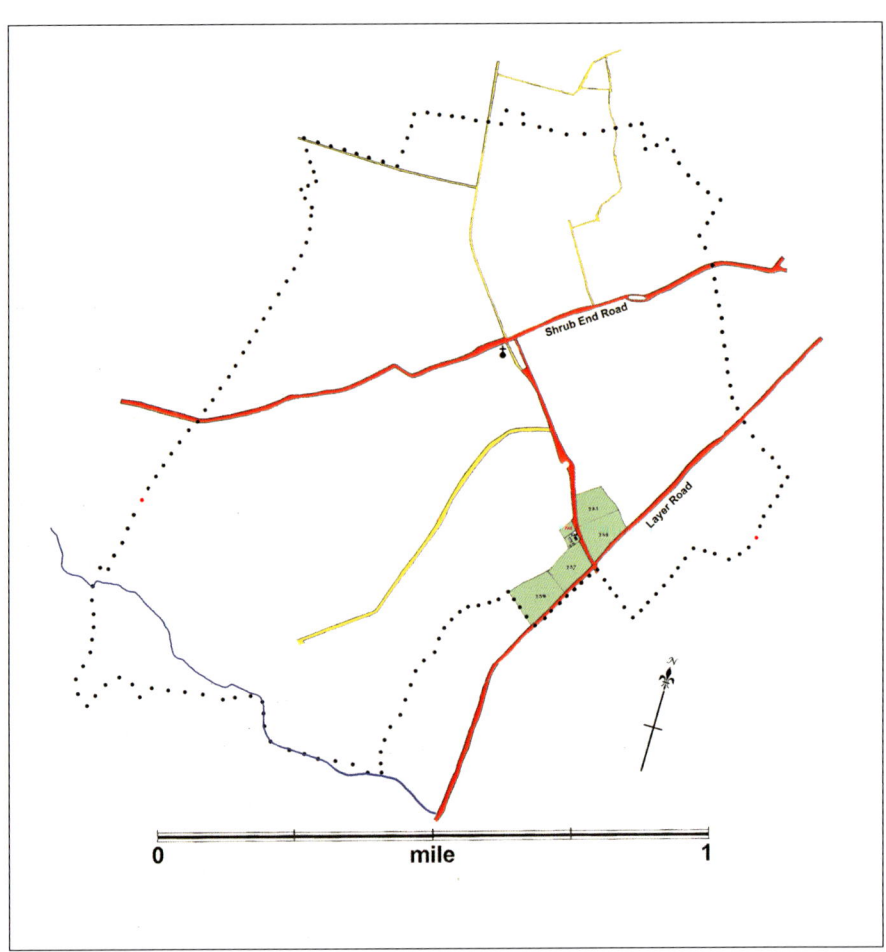

The tithe map of 1839 lists 5 fields totalling 30 acres belonging to the farm, which at the time was owned by the Trustees of the Magdalen Charity and farmed by Robert Hunt.

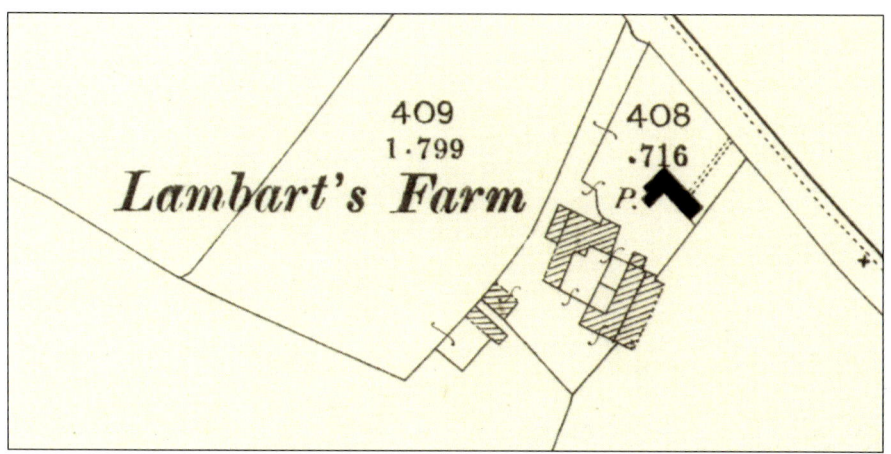

Lambert's (Lambart's) Farm buildings,
(P is for pump, situated at the rear of the farmhouse.)

This small farmhouse is situated on Gosbecks Road almost at the junction with Layer Road. It is well screened from the road but the style of its entrance hints at its history.

Everything about Lambert's is modest. It has never had a large acreage and the surviving building is a 1½ storey timber-framed structure with a mansard roof probably dating from the 17th century or possibly earlier.

In north-east Essex a roof with a double pitch on two sides and gable ends is called a mansard roof. The correct name for this type of roof is *gambrel* but this is seldom used in Essex. They have been a characteristic of many cottages and some larger houses in this part of the country since the early 17th century, and are incorrectly named

37

Christina Edwards

Lambert's (Lambart's) Farmhouse.

A typical mansard roof structure, with dormer.

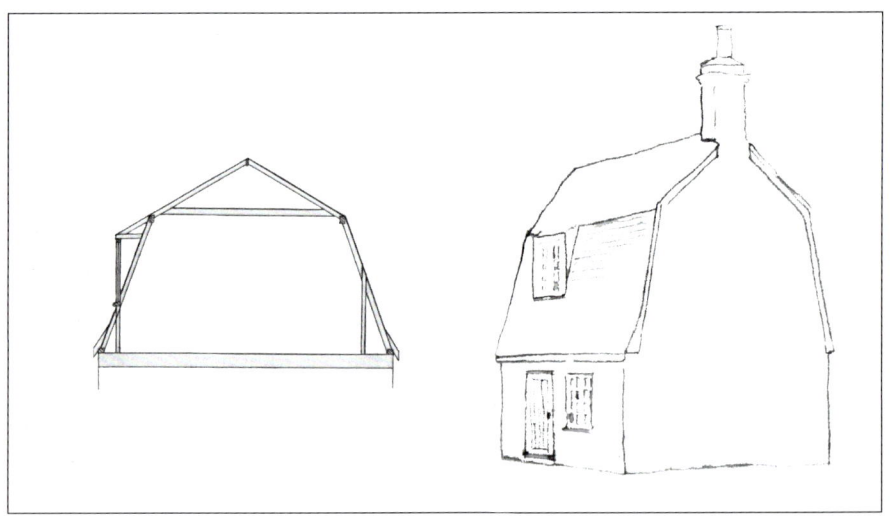

after the French architect François Mansard who popularized the use of the four-sided double pitch roof in France. It is uncertain how the mansard roof design arrived in Essex but of the various theories suggested my preference is that the design evolved locally as a way of increasing the headroom in the attic space of single storey dwellings and were not given the name, mansard until much later. This idea not only overcomes the problem that some of the cottages that display this style predate the French architect, it explains why such buildings are often described as being of 1½ storeys.

The name Lambart or Lambert first appears in the Stanway records in the 16th century and in the 18th century there was a John Lambart paying tithes to Stanway Rectory. Over the years the farmhouse has had several owners and occupiers. By 1839 it belonged to the Magdalen Charity. At this time the farm is recorded as having 30 acres (12 ha) and the farmhouse was being lived in by the Charity trustees' tenant, Robert Hunt who is described as a farmer. By 1851 the resident was James Sorrell also a farmer employing three labourers. Ten years later the farm was being run by James' widow, Barbara, and her 21 year-old son, Joseph. Barbara gives her occupation as 'Occupation of house' and each of her two sons is described as 'Farmer's son'. It seems likely the property was still owed by the charity. During this period the farm was sometimes referred to as Magdalen Farm or Hospital Farm.

The Colchester Hospital of Mary Magdalen was first established for leprous and infirm people in the reign of Henry I. It was run as

Lexden Morant

Lambart's as it could have looked when used as a farmhouse.

the charity of St Mary Magdalen and was re-established in 1610 after which it provided accommodation for a master and five poor single or widowed people of Colchester. The master was also the rector of St Mary Magdalen's church, which stood on the corner of Magdalen Street and Brook Street.

In 1837 the endowment of the charity consisted of over 50 acres (20 ha) of land within its parish and a similar area in the parish of Stanway. Some of this would have been Lambert's Farm. At various times up to 1932 all the land and houses owned by the charity, except the masters house and the almshouses, were sold and the proceeds invested.

During the early 1930s Lambert's farm was owned and worked by the Taylor family who grew mostly market garden produce. By 1939 the farmhouse was being lived in by four members of the Holditch family none of whom had any connection with agricultural activities.

It is seems likely Lambert's farmlands were being worked by either a market gardener who lived on another site, or by the adjoining Gosbecks Farm. In 1954 the owners of this farm purchased all Lambert's land to replace the land north of Gosbecks Road that it lost to Colchester Borough Council for residential and commercial development. Since this time Lambert's Farmhouse has been a private residence.

4 Magazine Farm

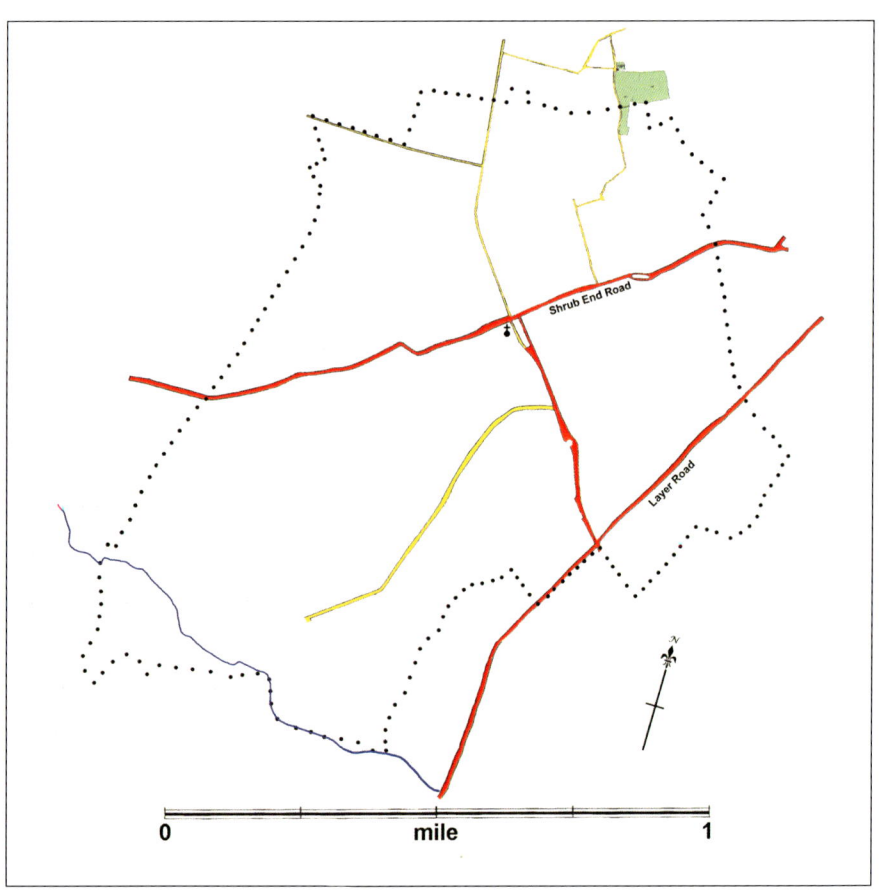

Only one field belonging to Magazine farm fell within the parish of Shrub End.
The farmhouse and most of its land was in Lexden.

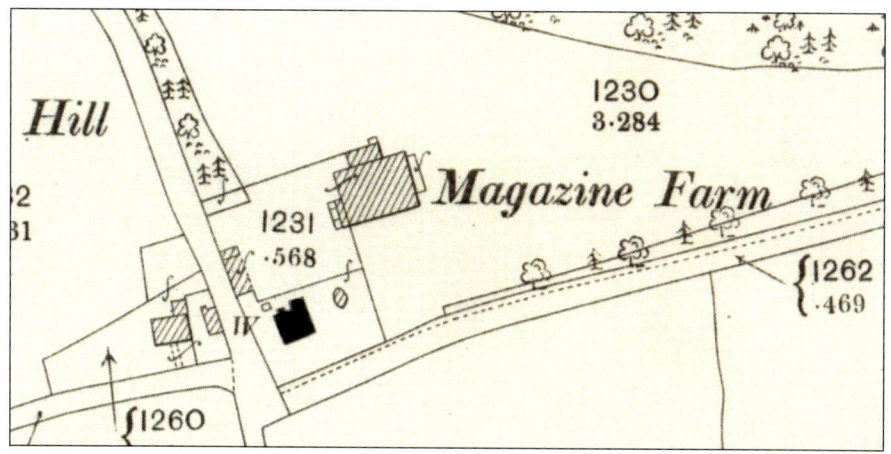

The original Magazine farmhouse was on north side of the public footpath/cycle way.
(W is for well).

The 1838 tithe map of the parish of Lexden indicates that the original Magazine Farm stood within the bounds of the Lexden Park estate and did not have any land in what was to shortly become the new parish of Shrub End.

A new Magazine farm and a farmhouse, which still stands, were built on the south side of the track at the top of what is now Parsons Hill in a field that had belonged to and was farmed by Samuel Phillips in 1838. By the time the new farm was built in 1902 it was owned by the trustees of the Errington Estate, who were the administrators of the former Lexden Park Estate, and farmed by George Blake.

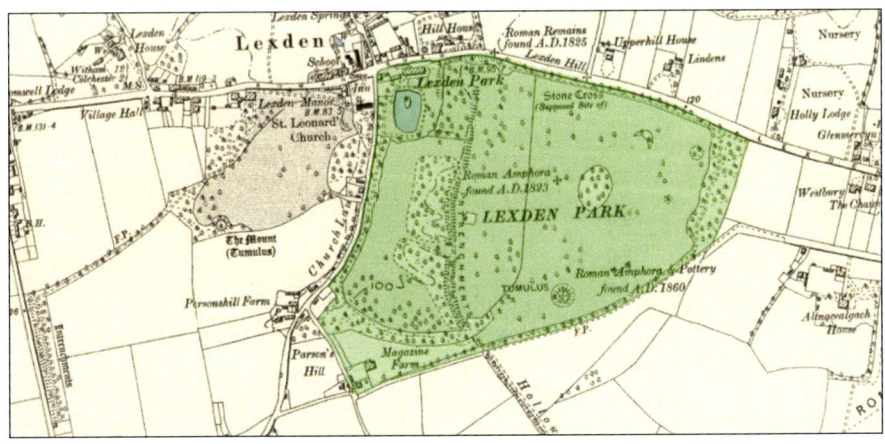

John Fletcher-Mills, a banker, acquired the Lexden Park Estate c1821. The tithe records of 1838 indicate the Park along with Magazine Farm and its lands (shown in green) were all in the hands of John Fletcher-Mills.

George Blake first appears in this area in the 1891 census when he was employed as a game keeper and farmer by the Lexden Park Estate and living at Game Keeper's Cottage near Bluebottle Grove, Park Road with his wife Amy and children: Amy, William, Mabel and Walter. Unfortunately his wife, Amy, died a couple of years later but by the time George had moved into the new Magazine Farmhouse he had a new wife, Agnes, and a growing family.

By 1911 George was a successful farmer. He died in 1922 leaving a substantial estate valued at £13,369 to his widow and children. In 1939 his widow and two of his unmarried daughters were still living in the Magazine farmhouse and his eldest son, William George, was living and working at the neighbouring Prettygate farm.

Some of the new Magazine Farm lands fell within the new parish of Shrub End and are now below a network of roads, one of which is Magazine Farm Way.

The new Magazine Farmhouse, built c1902. 2023

5 New House Farm

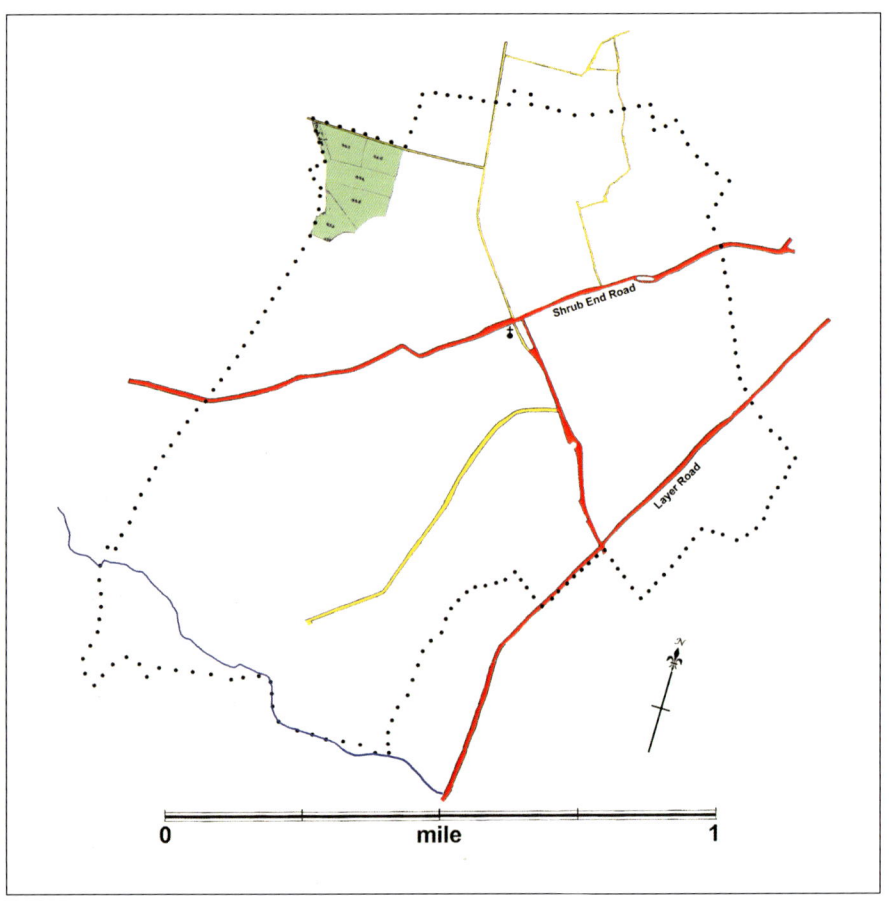

*New House farmlands lie in the north-west corner of the parish
to the north of Stanway Green.*

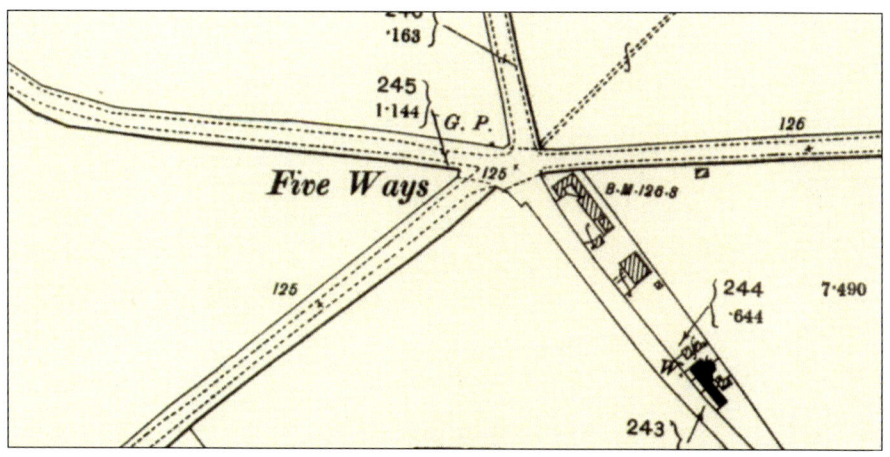

New House farm buildings, W is for well, situated close by the farmhouse.

This farm was created from a part of Stanway Heath when it was enclosed in 1791. It was divided into five enclosures, one of which is now open as Stanway Green. The total area of about 36 acres (14 ha) contained no buildings and was farmed by tenants of the owner, John Haynes Harrison of Copford.

By the time of the tithe assessment of 1839 the farm consisted of four fields totalling 31 acres owned by John Haynes Harrison and farmed by William Butcher. William is also recorded as the owner and occupier of a house and barn that had been built in the north-west corner of the northernmost field at Fiveways. The barn was demolished in 1997 to be replaced with bungalows. The late-Victorian, redbrick farmhouse house, now named *Fiveways Farmhouse* stands on the site of the 1840s

Fiveways Farmhouse on the site of the original farmhouse. 2022

Bramble Cottage and Long Hedges, mid 19th century cottages. 2022

farmhouse inhabited by the Butcher family. Close by are a pair of one-up-one-down cottages built by William Butcher for his farm workers sometime during the mid 19th century. They have since been extended and are now known as Bramble Cottage and Long Hedges. Apart from the Green all of the former farmland is now in use for residential, commercial or industrial purposes.

6 Oliver's Farm

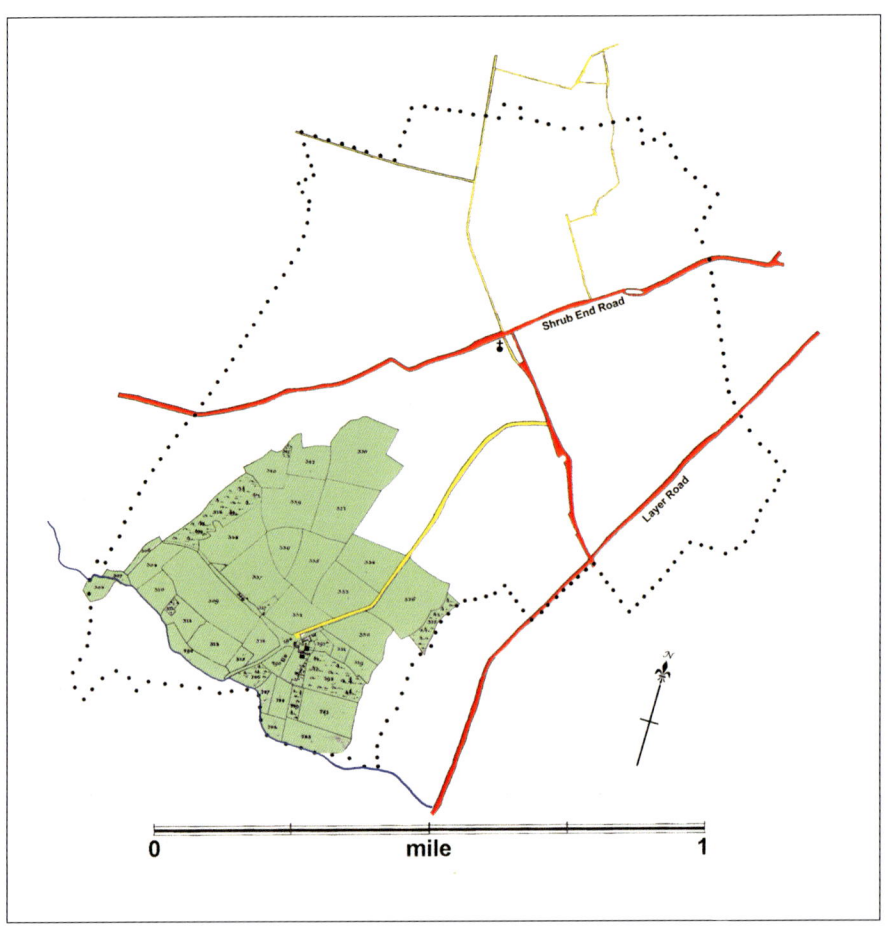

Oliver's, with 327 acres (131 ha) was one of the largest farms in the parish.

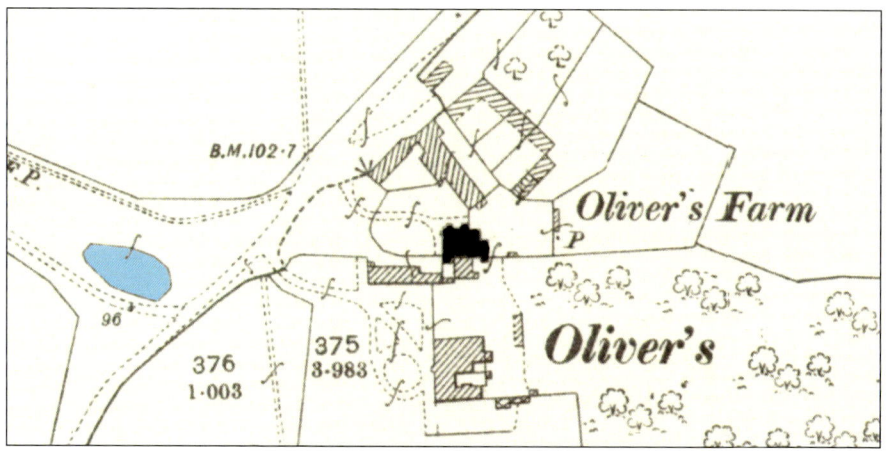

The pump (P) appears to have been shared with the mansion and is situated to the east of the farmhouse.

In the distant past Oliver's was a manor in its own right. It is thought to be named after Ralph Oliver, an early holder of the manor. It was still being referred to as the manor in 1564. On the site of the original manor house stands the existing Oliver's mansion. The building's elegant Georgian façade hides the remains of a timber-framed structure whose origins date back to the 15th century.

Close by the mansion stands the 16th century Oliver's farmhouse, now known as Little Oliver's. This was home to the tenant farmers who worked the estate. This has always been a sizable operation. In 1338 Oliver's was farming in excess of 170 acres. In 1817 the naturally infertile sandy soil needed heavy manuring, and this was supplemented with Colchester town muck making it some of the best land in the parish. The land was well farmed on a four-year rotation of, turnips, barley, clover, and wheat.

By the time of the 1839 tithe award Oliver's farmlands extended to a total of 327 acres (131 ha). This was a mixture of arable and pasture also including 14 acres (6 ha) of woodland.

Oliver's Mansion. 2013

The weatherboard Little Oliver's, formerly Oliver's Farmhouse. 2019

Oliver's pond with the once familiar hayricks in the background.
The barns to the right have been converted into houses. c1920

Christina Edwards

7 Plume Farm

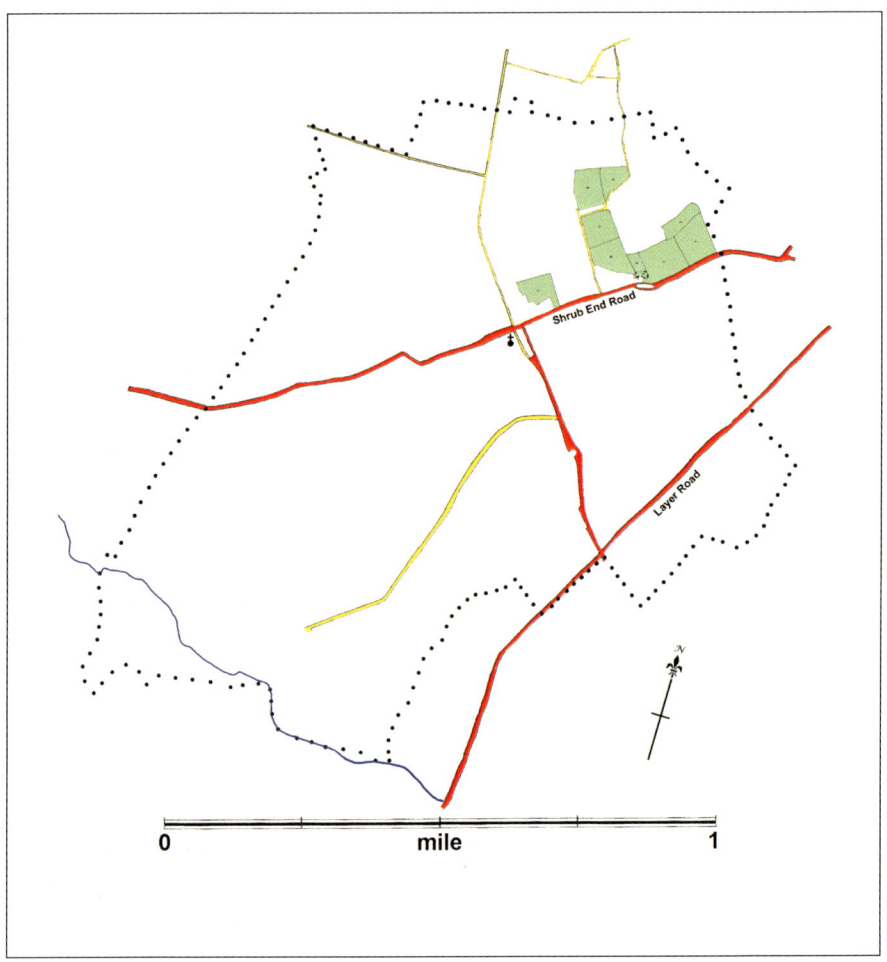

The 53 acres (21 ha) of farmland being farmed by Plume Farm in 1838.

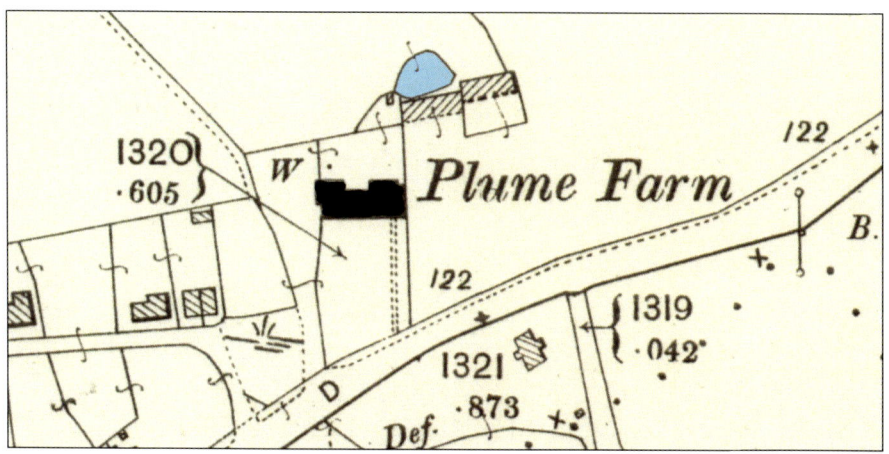

Plume farmhouse with the farm buildings and pond beyond the well. The orientation of the farmhouse is interesting and tends to indicate that, when it was built, what is now Pond Chase was a roadway leading onto what became Lexden Heath.

Plume Farm was located on Shrub End Road near the junction with Plume Avenue, a lasting reminder of its former existence. The farmhouse is remembered by some of the older residents and is thought to have dated from the 17th century. In 1838 it was occupied by Elizabeth Skitter who probably farmed the eight fields totalling 53 acres (21 ha), all arable, that made up the entire acreage of the farm.

It is thought this has never been a large farm and its documentary records are sparse but it is recorded on Chapman & André's map of 1777. There are however several 18th century Petty Session court records which indicate that the tenant farmer, Edmund Plume, could have been a difficult employer who was reluctant to part with his money.

55

In 1786 Plume was before the court for not paying Frances Beaumont the ten shillings and eight pence (53p) wages he owed her. Again in the same month Sarah Crookson claimed Plume had agreed to pay her three shillings and ten pence (19p) then refused to pay her.

The 19th century census returns indicate that the farm had ceased to operate as an independent entity and the farmhouse was used to accommodate two or more farm labourers and their families into the 20th century.

By the time this photo was taken in the 1920s the farmhouse had been in multiple occupancy for many years. It was demolished in 1939.

Bernard Polley

The 1805 OS 1" map showing Plume Farm and Pond Chase leading on to the track across Lexden Heath and into Lexden village

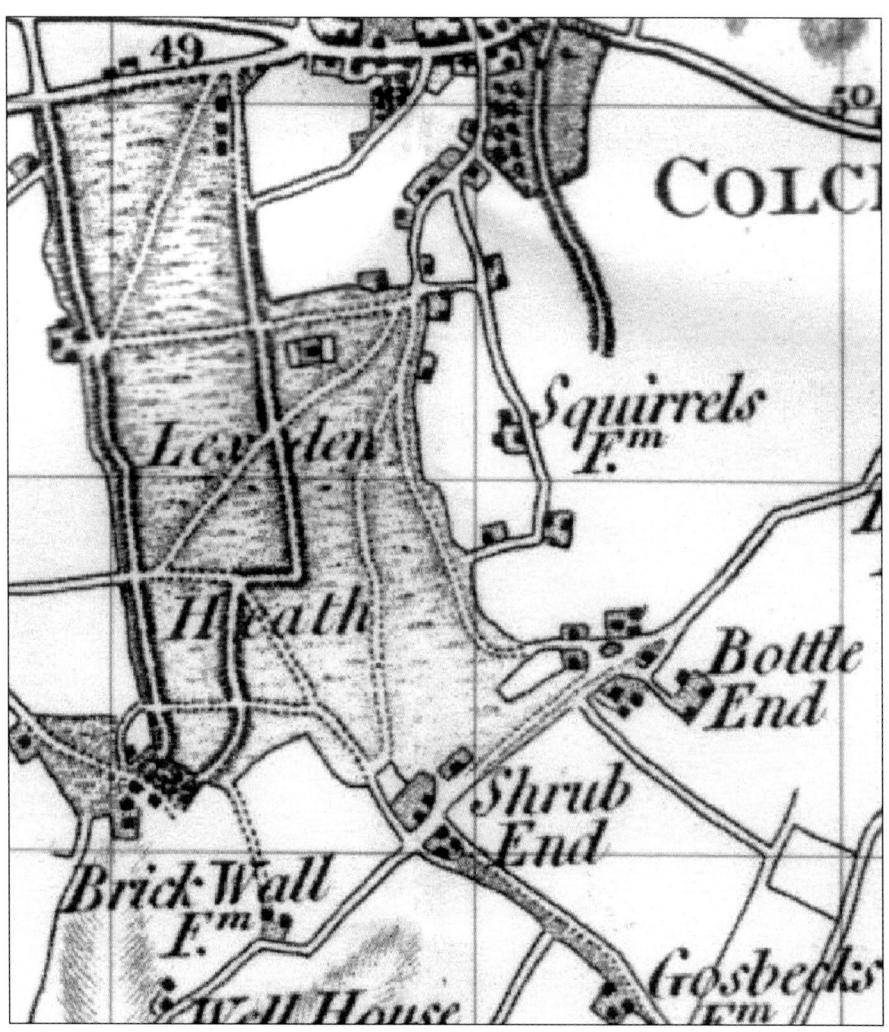

8 Prettygate Farm

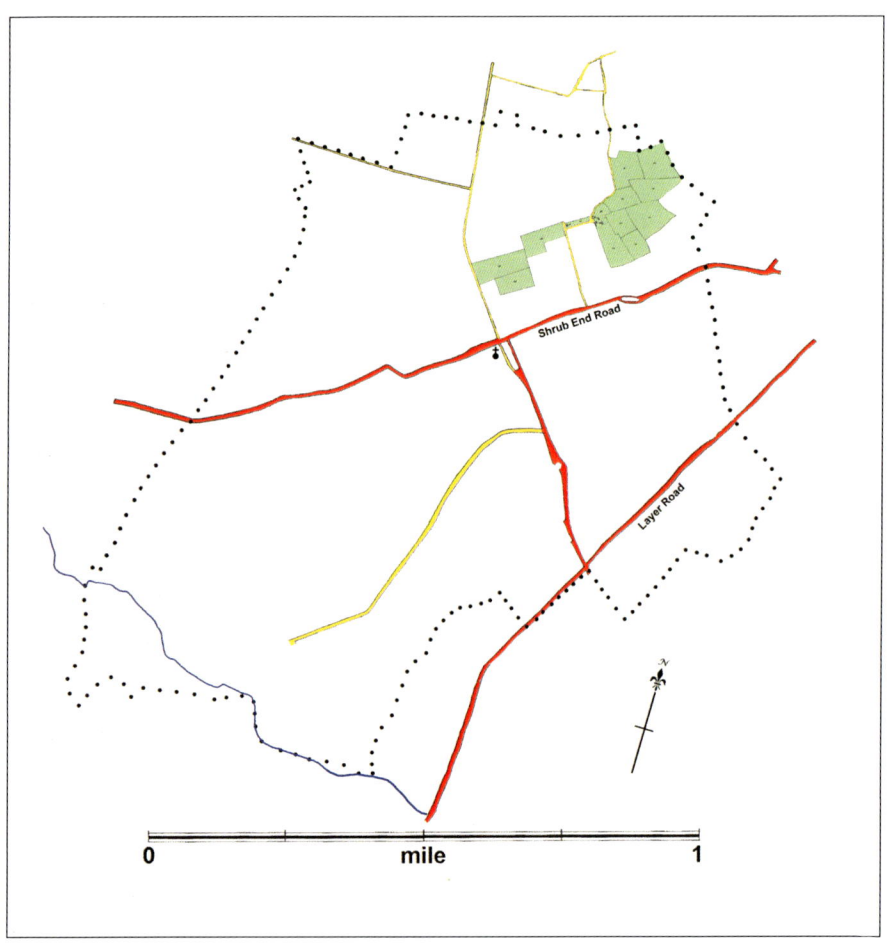

*The 1838 tithe records the farm was owned by Elizabeth Papillon
and its 54 acres (22 ha) were farmed by Thomas Gray.*

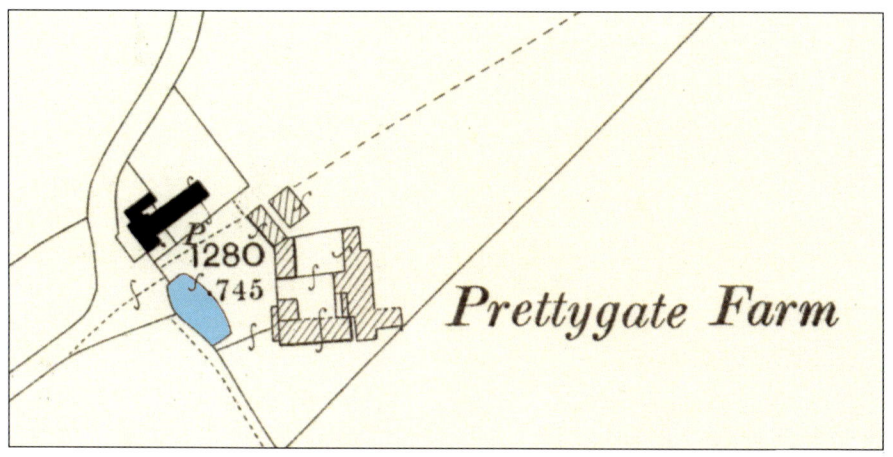

Prettygate farmhouse with the pump (P) between it and the pond.

Estate agents now describe Prettygate as a desirable area in the west of Colchester. It is largely a post WWII development on land that had belonged to several farms. One of these acquired a pretty gate in the early 19th century and the farm soon came to be named as Prettygate Farm.

The earliest record of this farm dates from 1655 when a house called *Coopers* in the parish of Lexden was described as being on an outlying farm. Several later references to either Coopers or Cowpers indicate that this was the farm that became known as Prettygate farm.

The early 1805 OS map shows an unnamed building on the site of Coopers farm and the Lexden tithe award map of 1838 indicates that the farmhouse on the site of what was to be Prettygate Farm was owned by Elizabeth Papillon of Lexden Manor, and occupied by Thomas Gray who farmed ten fields totalling about 54 acres (22 ha).

Bernard Polley

The farmhouse stood in what is now Prettygate Road just south of Prettygate shops. It was a substantial timber-framed building parts of which probably dated from the 16th or 17th century.

By 1851 the inhabitant of the farmhouse, recorded as Cowpers Farm, was George Phillips, a single man of 32 accompanied by a servant, Maria Taylor aged 44 and an 18 year-old labourer, James Humberlee. George described himself as a farmer of 188 acres employing 12 men and boys. George may well have been farming many acres on other farms. He was a member of a large farming family and was brought up on Malting Farm, another farm that belonged to Lexden manor and farmed by George's father, Samuel Phillips.

The farmhouse stood on the far side of the wide greensward in Prettygate Road. 2022

In 1861 the farm was again recorded as Cowpers with George Phillips, now aged 42, as the farmer. By now he had two servants, Sarah Keeble age 45 and Sarah Vickers age 15. George appeared to be a successful farmer as his acreage had increased to 270 acres and he was employing 11 men and 4 boys.

Mr Phillips was still there in 1871 in what was then called Coopers Farm along with Sarah Keeble, now described as housekeeper and another domestic servant, 16 year-old Mary Percival. Although the acreage he farmed had decreased to 215 acres George was still employing 11 men and 4 boys.

Particulars.

LOT 1 *(Colored Pink on Plan).*

THE VERY

Attractive Small Freehold Farm

"The Pretty Gate,"

Having a considerable and important Building frontage to King Harold Road.

COMPRISING

Brick Plaster-and-Tiled Residence

CONTAINING

Dining Room, facing South, with old oak beam.
Drawing Room, facing South and East.
Morning Room, facing West, with old oak beams and open grate.
Kitchen, with range, copper and oven.
Scullery, Larder, above which are
Five Bedrooms,
Lean-to brick and slated coal and wood houses and Conservatory, Outside Closet.
The Town Water is laid on.

The Farm Buildings

INCLUDE

Brick and slated Stables and Coach House, timber and slated Cattle Shed, brick, timber and thatched Barn with lean-to Piggeries, detached brick, timber and slated Cart and Implement Shed, timber and thatched Shed, Cattle Shed and Loose Box, timber and slated Poultry Houses and enclosed Yard,

TOGETHER WITH

75 acres   3 roods   7 poles

OF

Excellent Arable and Pasture Land

Prettygate Farm as described in
the sale document of 1923.

There appears to be no record of the Coopers Farm in the 1881 census but George Phillips has moved in with his brother Edmund at Malting Farm who describes himself as a farmer of 145 acres employing 8 men and 1 boy. George is now described as a 62 year-old 'Land Surveyor'.

Later census returns for the farmhouse indicate that its residents had little or nothing to do with running the farm. The land was probably being farmed from the adjoining Magazine Farm, which was occupied by the ambitious William Blake.

In 1922 William's father, George, died leaving an estate in excess of £13,300 which probably led to William's successful bid for Prettygate Farm when it was auctioned as lot 1, when parts of the Lexden manor lands and properties were sold.

William Blake appears in both Kelly's and Benham's directories with his address as Prettygate Farm from 1929 until 1950 when the entry changes from W S Blake to G S Blake. This was George Samuel, eldest son of William George and Winifred. The last directory entry for G S Blake at Prettygate Farm was in 1956.

Shortly after this Colchester Borough Council acquired the farm, and all the farm buildings were demolished to make way for the Prettygate Estate of 1750 new homes. The only part of the farm to survive was the gate, which for many was displayed at the Prettygate pub.

The 'pretty gate' made by local farmer, William Baines in the early 19th century.

Bernard Polley

9 Rayner's Farm

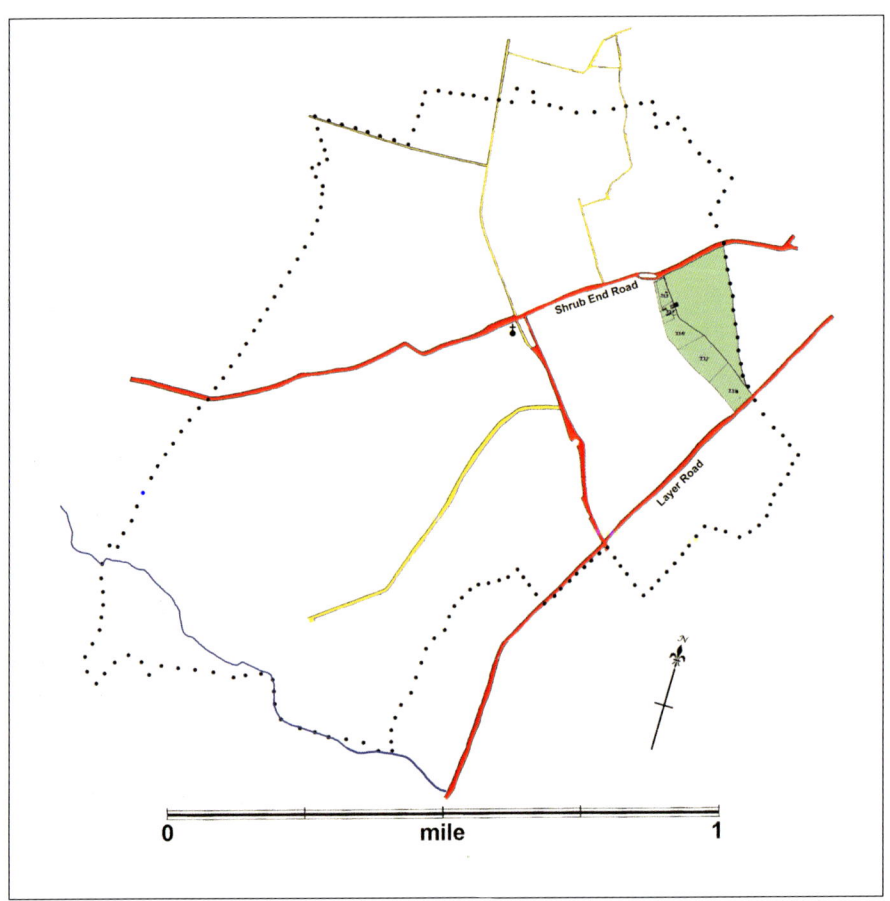

Rayner's Farm lands in the parish of Shrub End. Prior to the formation of this parish some of the farm's land was in the parish of Stanway and some in the parish of St Mary at the Walls and some in Lexden giving it a total in excess of 60 acres (24 ha).

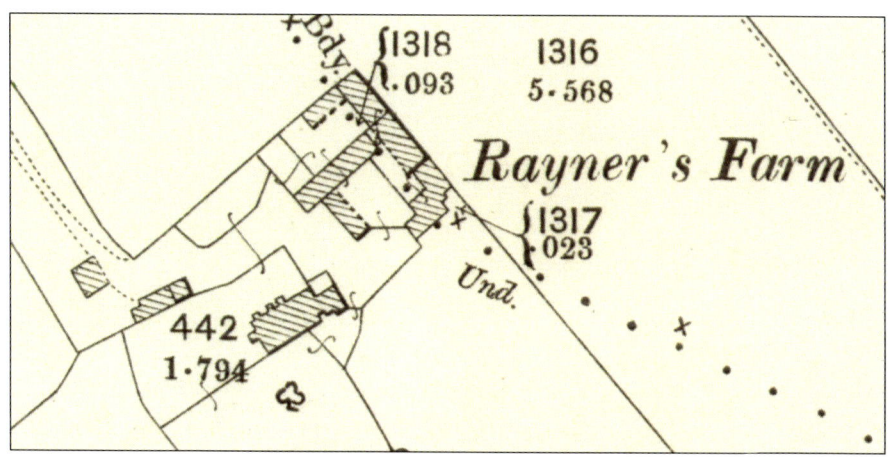

Rayner's farm buildings.

The histories of Rayner's and Walnut Tree Farms are inextricably linked. The farmhouses are within a stone's throw of each other and for many years their lands have been owned or farmed by the same people.

The early records are difficult to interpret as both farms held land in Stanway, Lexden, and Colchester. There were frequent disputes between the three authorities leading to the same land being recorded in different parishes at varying times.

In 1668 Thomas Clare, the Stanway Yeoman, considered the whole of Shrub Oak Farm, later to be named Rayner's Farm, was in Lexden and within the liberties of Colchester.

By 1700 it had been agreed the farmhouse, orchard, and somewhere between 10 and 20 acres [4-8 ha] of land were within the parish of Stanway, leaving a considerable acreage of its land in Lexden and Colchester.

The Chapman & André map of Essex, published in 1777 and surveyed between 1772 and 1774, shows an unlabeled building on the site of Rayner's Farm as being less than 100 yards (90 metres) from another unlabelled building on the site of what was to become Walnut Tree Farm.

Thomas Clare left the farm to his grandson, William Rayner, whose descendants continued to hold the farm for centuries. The Rayners seemed to be quite short lived and several generations later in 1782 a widowed Mary Rayner married her bachelor neighbour, Benjamin Firmin, of what was to become Walnut Tree Farm.

From then on the histories of the two farms become somewhat entangled but were not legally united until both were bought by the trustees of the Errington Estate in 1846.

The more recent history of Rayner's Farm is included with that of Walnut Tree Farm. (page 76)

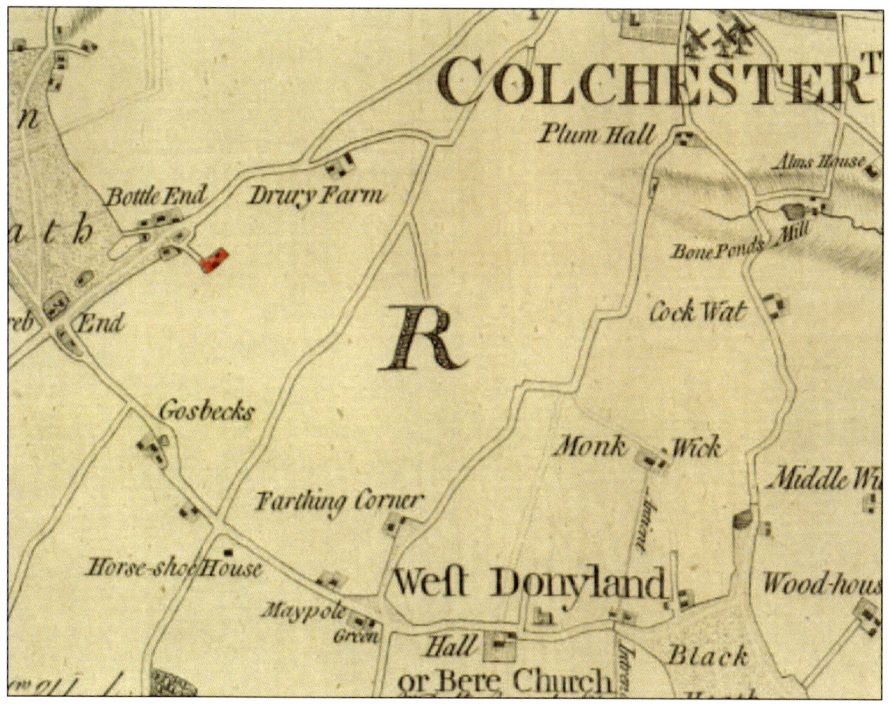

The Chapman & André map showing the unlabeled Rayner's farm here highlighted in red.

10 Squirrels Farm

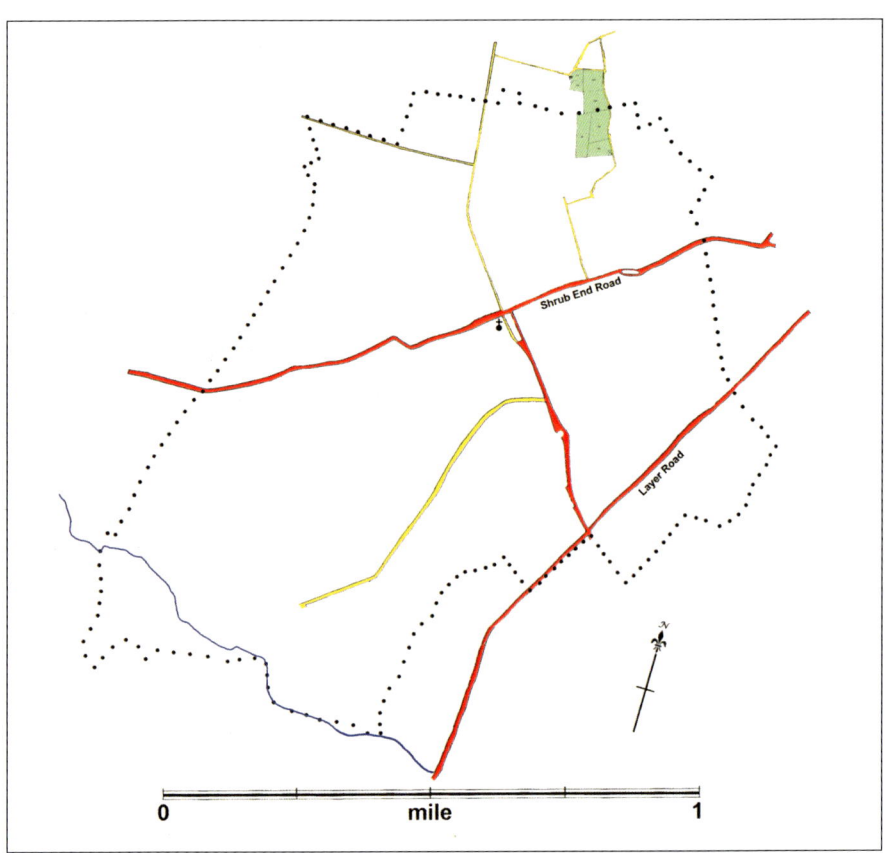

Squirrels Farm does not feature in the 1838 Lexden tithe documents but it was located on plot 82 in the south-east corner of the fields coloured green. It, along with the other fields shown in green, were owned and farmed by James Baines whose farmhouse was outside the parish in the north-west corner of the farmlands.

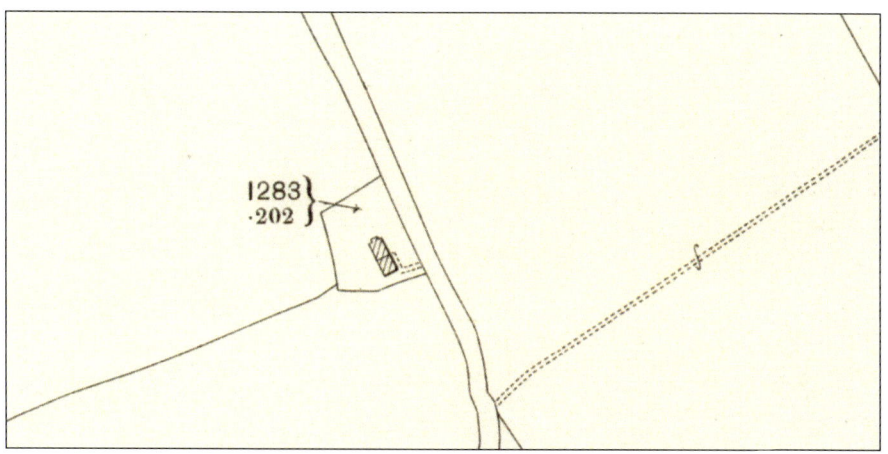

*Squirrels Farmhouse building is all that remained by the time of
the earliest OS survey for their 25 inch edition.*

The only record of Squirrels Farm appears on the 1805 1"(one inch)
OS map. It is shown as three buildings located on the west side of
what is now Prettygate Road in the vicinity of numbers 83-91. Despite
extensive searches there appears to be no other surviving records of
this farm. A plot with an unnamed building on it appears on some
1877 and 1888 OS maps but by the time of the 1921 survey for the
1924 edition the site is shown as an empty plot.

It would appear that the section of what is now Prettygate Road
between the top of Parsons Hill and Prettygate Farm was known as
Squirrels Lane long after the disappearance of Squirrels Farm. The
Lexden census return for 1851 records a dwelling on the lane between
Magazine Farm and Cowpers Farm (later Prettygate Farm). The

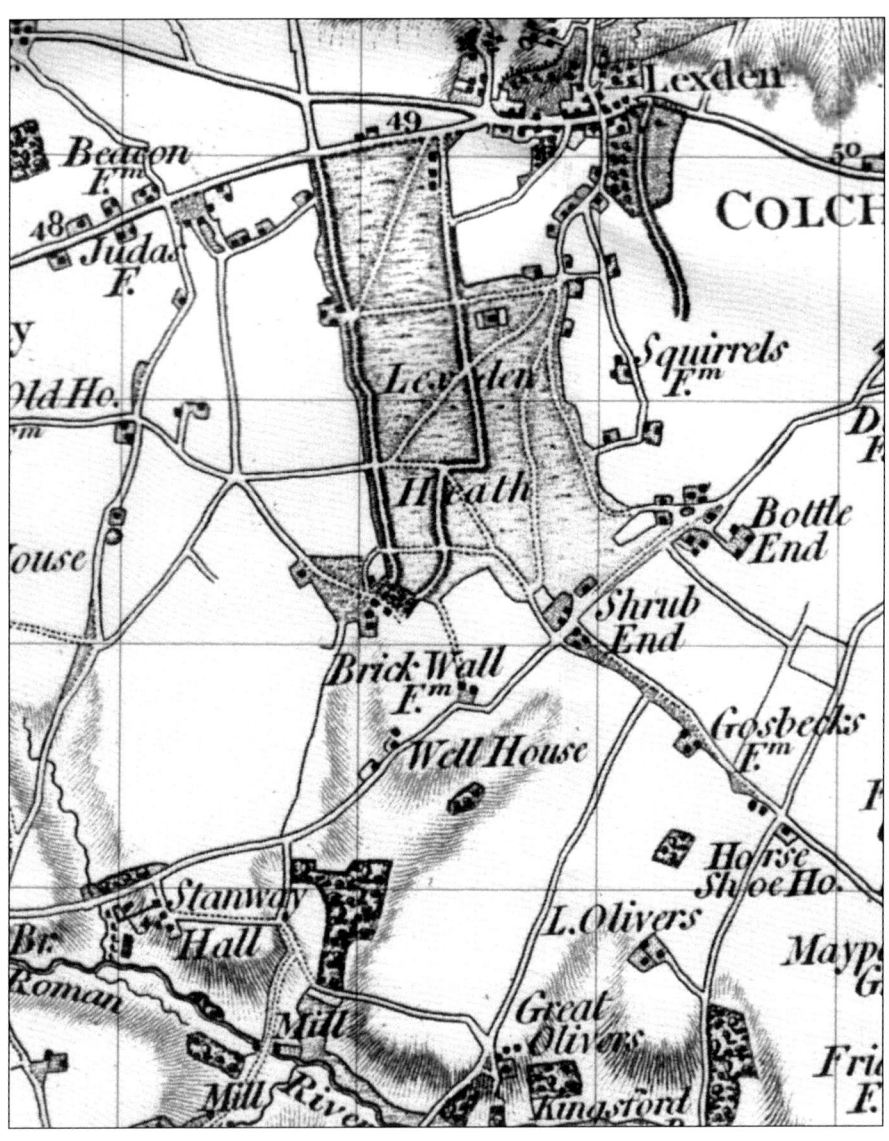

The earliest OS 1 inch edition of 1805 is the only map to show Squirrels Farm.

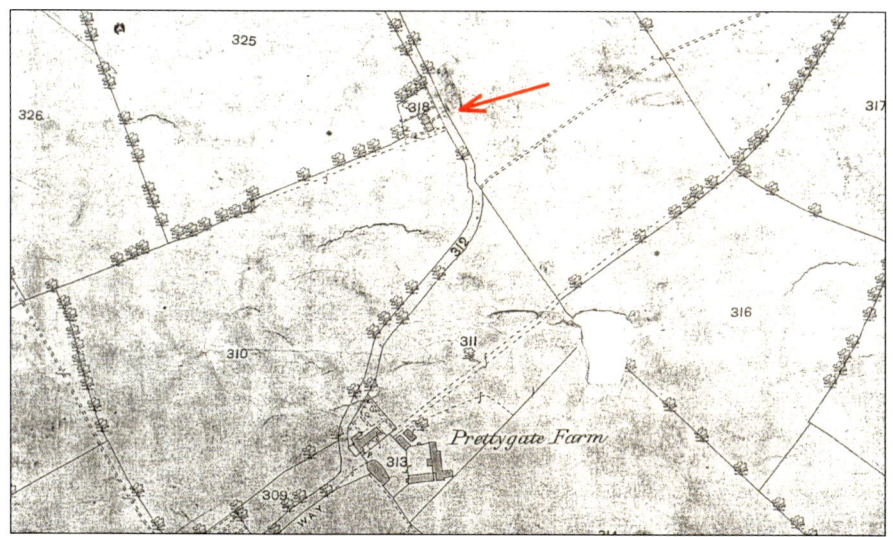

The OS 1ˢᵗ edition 25" map of 1870 shows an unlabelled single building divided into two at the location of Sqirrels Farm just north of Prettygate Farm

dwelling is recorded as being located in Squirrels Lane and is occupied by William Howe, a farm labourer, his wife and seven children. Subsequent census returns show multiple occupancy of the building. In 1891 it was occupied by two families consisting of a total of fourteen individuals.

The 1838 tithe map of Lexden shows the building and plot 82 in Squirrels Lane was owned by the farmer, James Baines, who also owned the adjoining fields 84 and 86 and several other nearby fields. At the time of the tithe assessment the Squirrels dwelling was occupied by William Howe and John Warren, presumably the same William Howe who was still in residence for the 1851 census.

71

11 Stanway Hall Farm

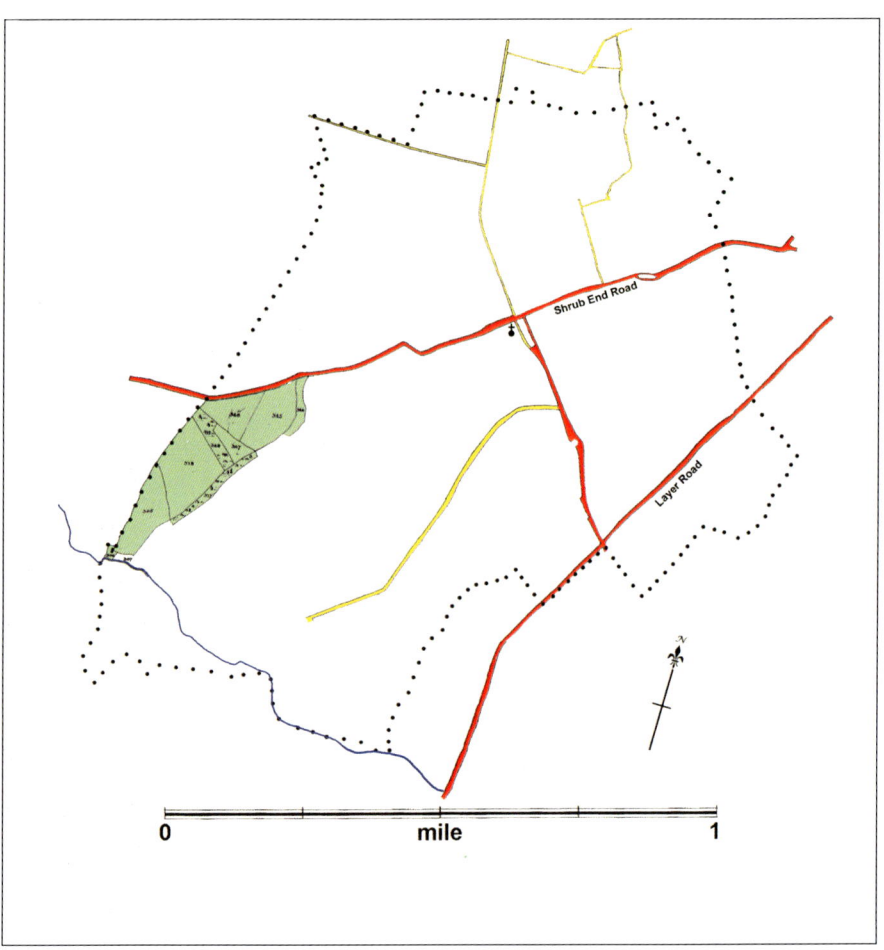

In 1839 the Stanway Hall Farm lands extended considerably into neighbouring parishes.

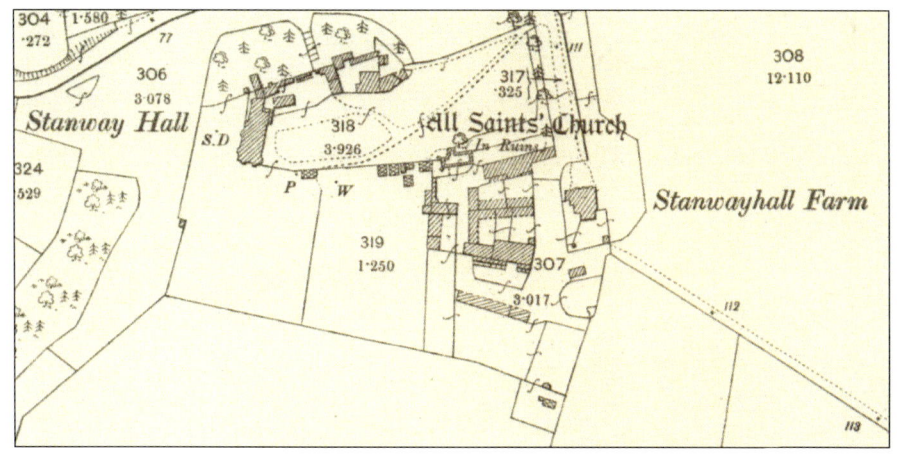

Stanway Hall and Stanway Hall Farm buildings.

This farm is situated on the southern edge of the ancient parish of Great Stanway or Stanway Magna close by the former manor house and the ruins of the original Stanway church of All Saints, now the site of Colchester Zoo. The farm and the Hall remained in the same ownership until the end of WWII when the farm and the Hall along with its grounds were sold separately.

The 19th century brick-built farmhouse is not within the bounds of the parish of Shrub End but a small proportion of its extensive lands lie within the parish. In 1839 these amounted to some 72 acres (28 ha) about half of which was woodland. These lands extended from Maldon Road down to Roman River and adjoined those of Oliver's. In 1839 they were all owned by John DeHorne and were being farmed by Harvey Foster.

The existing Stanway Hall Farmhouse is the latest of many built on this site. This late 19th century building of gault brick laid in Flemish bond was originally a symmetrical double fronted structure. It has since been extended to the south and west. 2019

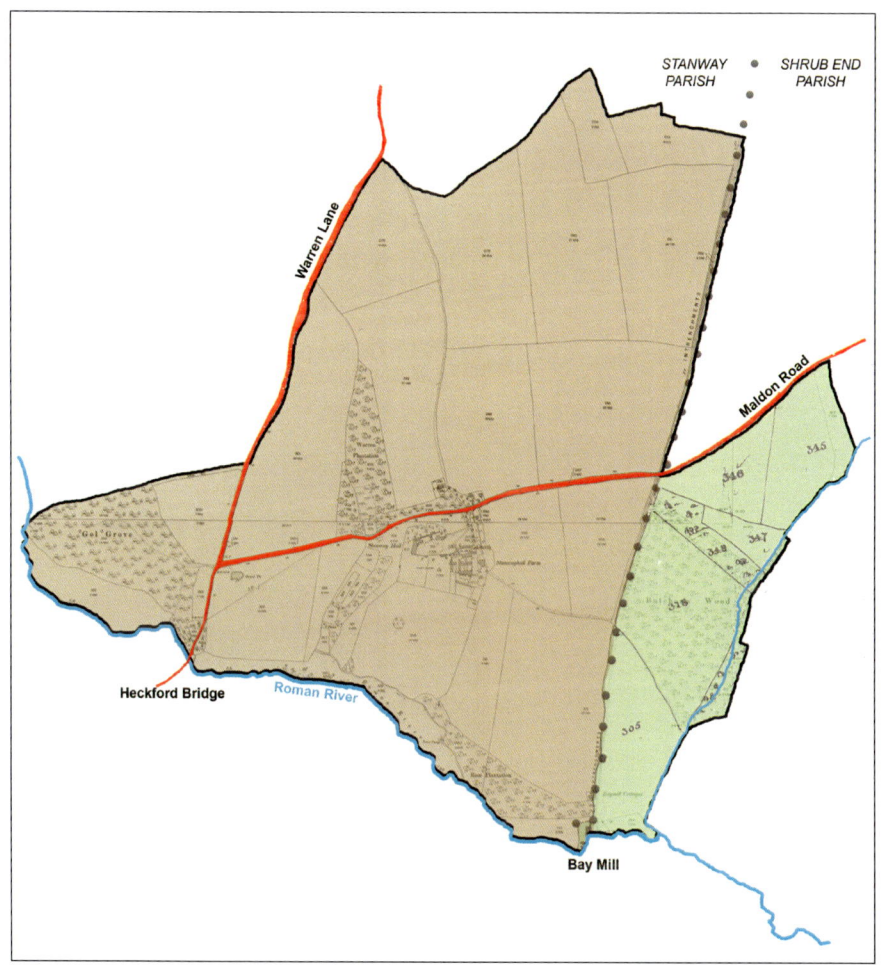

Stanway Hall Farm lands. The green area lies within the parish of Shrub End but the majority, coloured brown is in the neighbouring parish of Stanway. c1840

12 Walnut Tree Farm

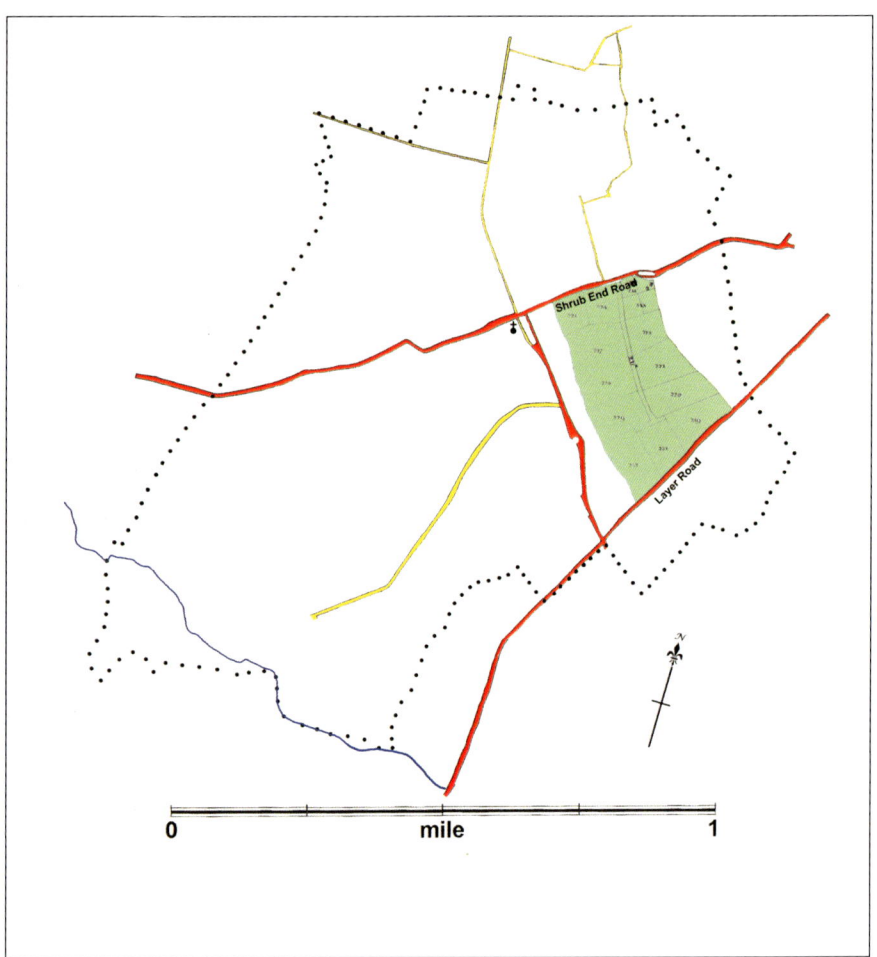

Walnut Tree Farm lands. 1839

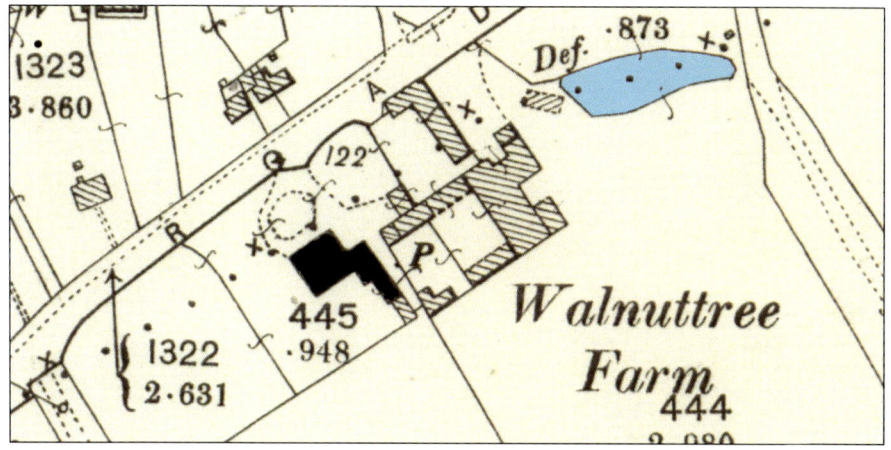

The Victorian farmhouse is the rectangular block above 445.
The older timber-framed structure is attached to this with the 'P' (pump) at its back.

Walnut Tree Farmhouse was a house of two parts; an ancient timber-framed building parts of which probably dated back to the 15th century, and a smart double-fronted early Victorian dwelling facing the highway. It would appear from the early editions of OS maps that the earlier course of the road ran closer to the farmhouse through a pond, a route still indicated by the parish boundary. Both road and boundary had little relevance to the running of the farm. Its early lands were nearly all on the Lexden side and remained so until Shrub Wood was cleared. This wood amounted to 117 acres (47 ha) when it was sold by John Stevens to William Talcott around 1697. Then sometime later it was bought by Thomas Blackman who cleared the wood to create a 'pretty farm'.

Christina Edwards

The new Walnut Tree Farmhouse.

Note the circular lawn, shown clearly on the 1870 OS map of the farm. c1900

This was certainly after 1713 when Rayner's farmland was described as 'abutting on Shrub Wood'. And before 1754 when John Moore was paying tithes on this former woodland as well as Shrub Walnut Farm, and Shrub Oak Farm. It seems likely that from around this time the two farms were being run as one. Then in 1782 Mary Rayner of Rayner's Farm married her neighbour, Benjamin Firmin of Walnut Tree Farm. When the new parish of Shrub End was created in 1845 the two farms were listed as Shrub Farm A and Shrub Farm B but, as mentioned

Christina Edwards

The ancient timber-framed Walnut Tree Farmhouse
to which the new one was attached.

earlier, the two farms were not legally united until both were bought
by the trustees of the Errington Estate in 1846.

The unification of Shrub Wood, Shrub Oak Farm, and Shrub
Walnut Farm may have inadvertently recreated an area of land not
dissimilar to the ancient manor of Shrebb. The total acreage of the
recombined areas as recorded in the tithe returns of the 1830s was
about 180 acres; the same as that of the manor of Shrebb held by
John Doreward Esq in 1496, as recorded by Philip Morant. This raises

the possibility of one or other or both Rayner's and Walnut Tree farmhouses being on the site of the Shrebb manor house. Nothing is known of the early history of Rayner's but parts of the timber-framed Walnut Tree farmhouse date back to the time of the last records of Shrebb manor.

Walnut Tree House. 2023

The combined farm soon came under the stewardship of the Folkard family. This family farmed in several parishes in north-east Essex and William Folkard moved into Walnut Tree Farm in 1854 and lived there until his death in 1911. His son, William Folkard the younger, then moved into the farm where he remained until his death in 1930. During the municipal boundary changes of 1934 the farm was transferred from the parish of Stanway into Colchester. Shortly after this the farmlands were acquired by the town, but William's daughter, Naomi, continued to live in the farmhouse until that too was bought by Colchester Borough Council in 1945 and converted into a care home.

Post WWII the Council started building the Shrub End Estate and created Walnut Tree Way that ran by the south side of the converted farmhouse, which was demolished a few years later to be replaced by a purpose built care home, Walnut Tree House. This underwent radical renovation in 2006 and is now a Colchester Council retirement home of nineteen one and two bedroom flats.

13 Well House Farm

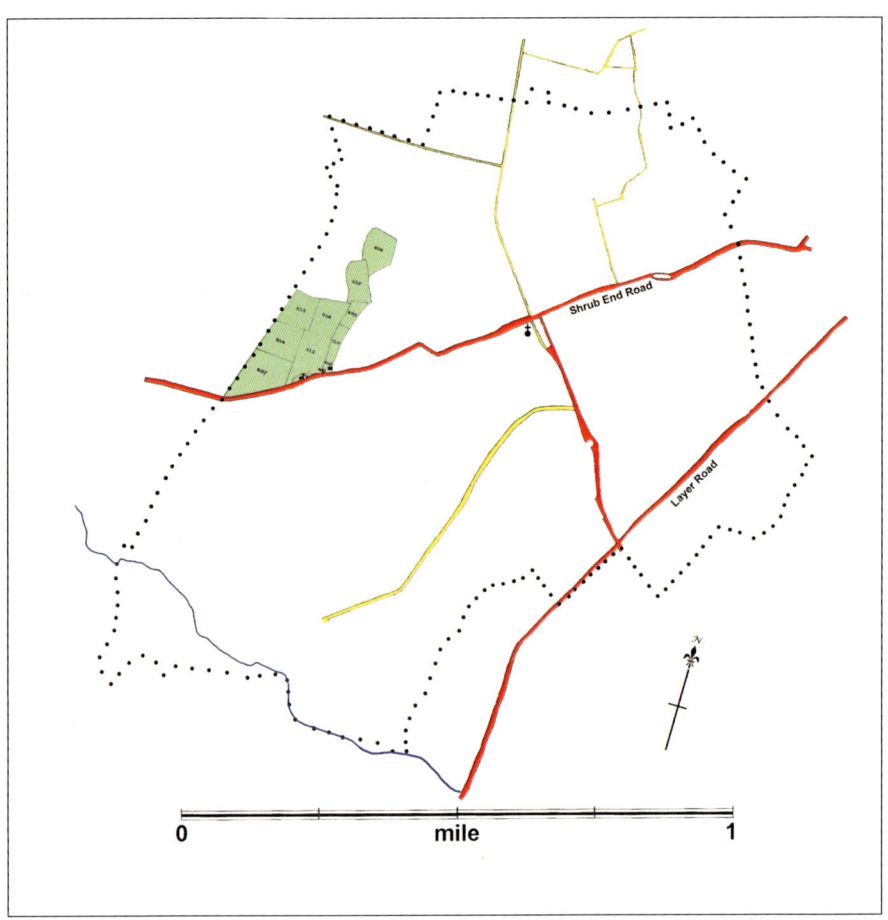

In 1839 all Well House fields were owned by Elizabeth Woodward and were being farmed by her husband William Woodward.

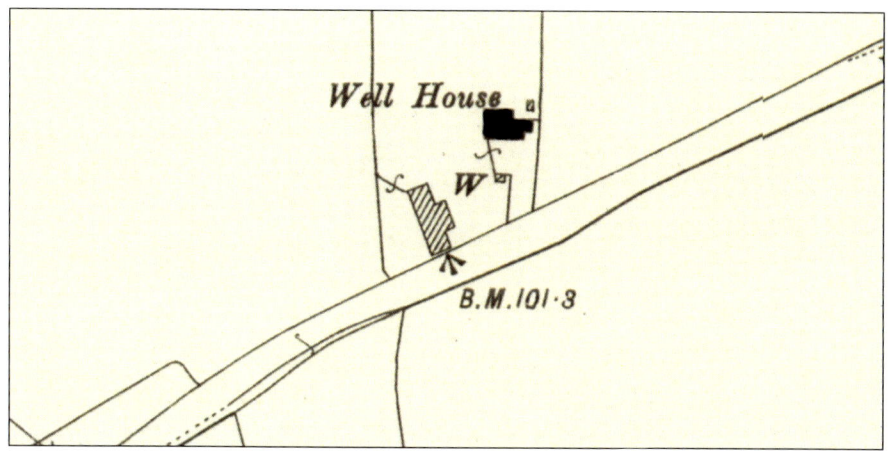

Well House Farm buildings as recorded in 1839.

Well House Farm is situated on the Colchester to Maldon Road about half way between All Saints' Church, Shrub End and Stanway Hall Farm. It lies at the western extremity of the parish of Shrub End. The farmhouse is of a size and design similar to Lambert's. The building is thought to date from the mid 17th century and now although much extended it still displays a fine mansard roof.

Records of this farm go back to the early 18th century when it was known as Haws. There was a field by this name on the opposite side of the road along with another known as Well field. By the mid 18th century these together with the messuage (cottage with garden) were referred to as Wellhouse. There appears to have been considerable changes to the size and boundaries of the farm during the following years. These were due to various sales and purchases along with several

Well House Farm. c1950   *Well House Farm. 2022*

inheritances from and to the owners and occupiers of the neighbouring Wiseman's Farm and Brickwall Farm.

By the time of the Tithe assessment in 1839 the farm was made up of ten fields plus the house and yard totalling some 44 acres (17½ ha). The whole was recorded as being owned by Elizabeth Woodward and farmed by William Woodward.

From this peak in the size of its acreage it was gradually reduced to that of a smallholding. In 1948 the cottage along with two fields totalling 2 acres (0.8 ha) was advertised as suitable for poultry and goat keeping. The house was described as being double-fronted, detached, built in brick, part boarded with tiled mansard roof and dormer windows, with brick-built, boarded and felted lean-to.

The property was next sold in 1969 when it was described as being about 300 years old with many exposed beams. Extensively renovated standing in a well-stocked, large garden with a hand-operated pump, several outbuildings, an orchard and about 1½ acres (0.6 ha) allowed to grow wild.

WELL HOUSE

Lexden Morant

Well House as it could have looked when used as a farmhouse.

14 Wiseman's Farm

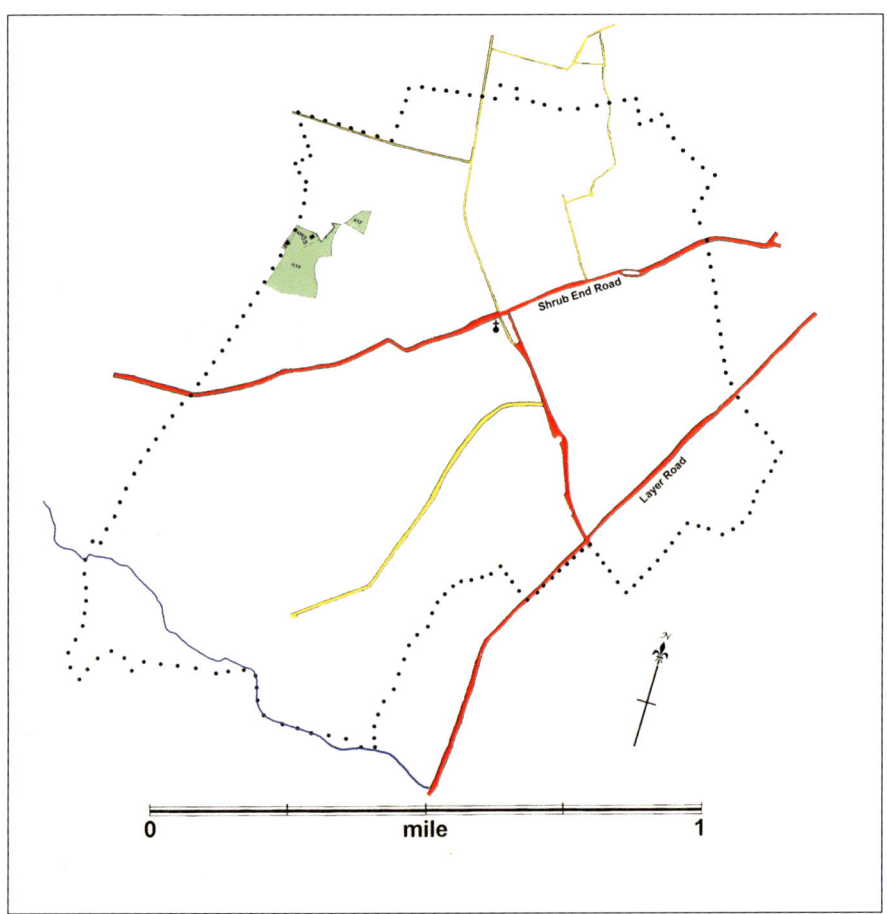

Wiseman's Farm lies on the south side of Stanway Green. At the time of the 1839 tithe it extended to over 40 acres (26 ha) but about half of this was outside the parish of Shrub End.

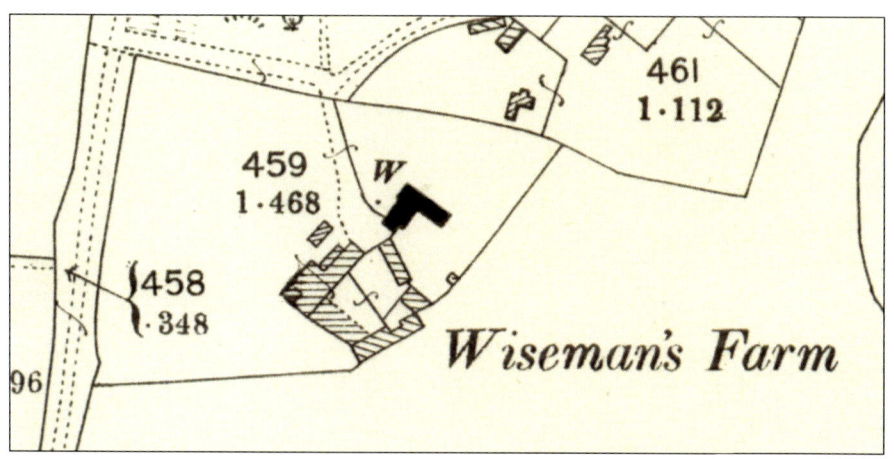

Wiseman's farm buildings, the farmhouse is by the well (W).

There are two Wiseman's Farms in the parish of Stanway, one on the London Road and the other at Stanway Green, which is now in the ecclesiastical parish of Shrub End. It has always been a small farm as shown by a record from the 17th century that refers to the farm's 12 acres (4.8 ha).

The listed Farmhouse is an early 18th century structure incorporating much material from an earlier 16th century building. It is timber-framed and plastered under a pantiled roof and is situated on the south side of the green.

Its former fields are now designated heritage land, as it is claimed they contain evidence of ancient habitation.

Chris & Melvyn Joscelyne

Wiseman's Farmhouse. c1970.

Wiseman's Farmhouse 2022

All Saints' Church, Stanway, Colchester.

Bernard Polley

Although this picture postcard of Shrub End dates from 1906 little would have changed since the church was built in 1845 shortly after the beginning of the Victorian era.
The white cottage by the church was demolished to make way for the War Memorial. The other cottage, now called Church Cottage has had many uses and still stands.
On the extreme right is the Leather Bottle inn sign standing in its garden, now the pub car park.

CHAPTER 4

The Victorian Village

Queen Victoria reigned from 1837 until 1901. This chapter looks at the many changes and events that took place in Shrub End during this period. It has already been mentioned that the parish was not created until 1845 with the building of All Saints' church. During the following few years the parish acquired a village green, windmill, school, and a reading room. In short, all the elements of the quintessential English village. Unfortunately they never formed a particularly picturesque group; nevertheless they each fulfilled their individual functions and helped bind the community through times of great change. During the Victorian era the population of the parish remained remarkably static at around 500 who were all housed in just over 100 dwellings. Most of these were clustered around the church at Bottle End and at the group of three farmsteads, Plume, Rayner's, and Walnut Tree collectively known as Shrub End. There were also a few isolated houses and a small cluster at Stanway Green.

Although the building of All Saints' church was the first Church of England place of worship to be built in Shrub End it was preceded by a few years by a non-conformist chapel built in what was soon to be

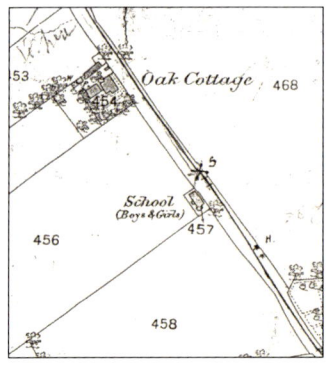 

above left: Extract from the OS 1st Ed 1841 map showing the building in King Harold Road as a school 'School (Boys & Girls)

above right: Built about 1840 to be used as a Congregational Chapel and School, which it continued to do until about 1954 when these activities were transferred to the new United Reformed Church in Plume Avenue. After this, the chapel became the Jesus Centre until about 2010 since when it has been the Lifehouse. 2022

called Chapel Road and is now King Harold Road. The chapel was funded and staffed by members of Lion Walk Congregational Church in Colchester. It is not clear precisely when this opened. It could have been as early as 1839 but was certainly being used for divine worship, as a Sunday school, and day school by 1843, which a little later was recorded as educating about 30 pupils.

All Saints' church is an impressive structure. It was designed by the eminent Victorian architect George Russell French. The original building consisted of a chancel, nave and tower surmounted by a splay-foot spire, all in the Decorated style in redbrick with stone dressings. The whole structure proportioned to suit its rural village location.

Bernard Polley

All Saints', Shrub End, built in 1845.

It was built in 1845 and carried on the name of All Saints', Stanway until 1960 when changes in the parish boundaries and the building of the dual-purpose church of St. Cedd in 1955 made it more appropriate to rename it All Saints', Shrub End.

Apparently the church was built 'at the earnest request of the inhabitants, which amounted to just over 500 and with the sanction and approbation of the Bishop of London although one wonders if the church authorities were spurred into action by the appearance of the nearby non-conformist chapel. The new church was to have 286 sittings, 202 of which were to be free, also it was proposed to build a vicarage as well as a schoolroom on the site. The total cost was calculated

All Saints', Shrub End. 2022

to be £2,150 of which upwards of £1,700 was subscribed by the more immediate encouragers of the undertaking with the balance raised by voluntary donations. An income for the vicar was provided from various endowments totalling £188 per year. This was probably quite a good income for the incumbent who also had the benefit of an attractive new vicarage. The schoolroom was not built until later and was erected on a different site.

Many Shrub End residents will be surprised to find they have a village Green, It is hidden away on the edge of the parish and is now known as Stanway Green even though it lies within the ecclesiastical parish of Shrub End. In Victorian times it was called Butcher's Green, after a family that had farmed much of the surrounding land. The Green is the last remnant of the once extensive heath that had been enclosed in 1791. The Green itself was part of this enclosure but was soon abandoned as uneconomical to farm, probably due to the number of earthworks created by much earlier inhabitants of the area. It remained the property of the descendant of the original owner of the enclosure until 1963 when it was purchased by Colchester Borough Council who registered it as a village green.

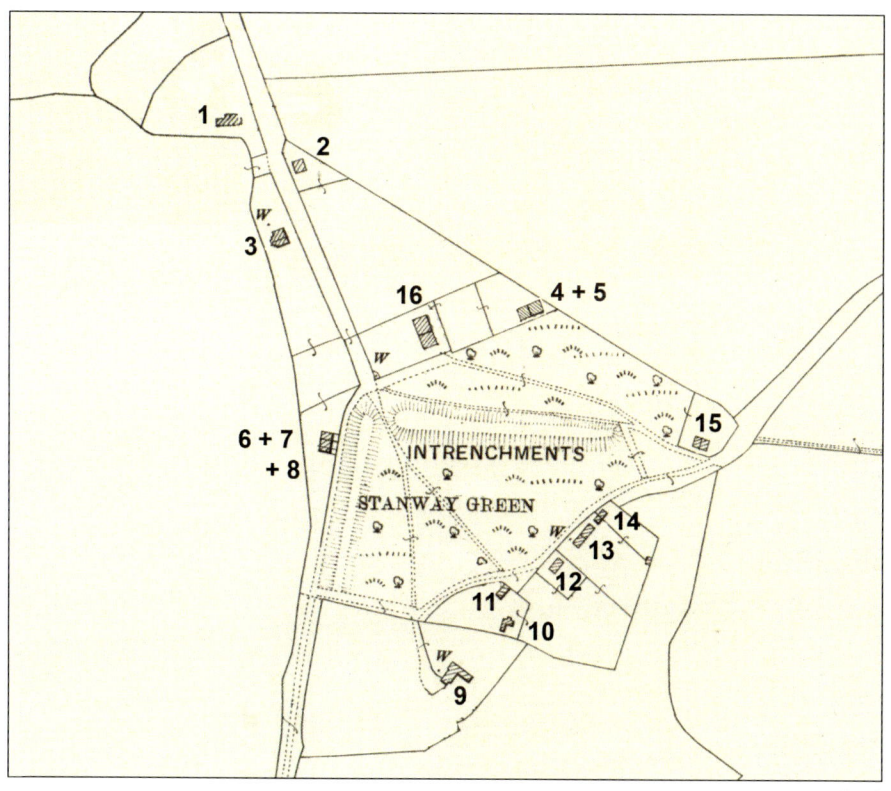

Some of the buildings that existed in Stanway Green during Victorian times.

1	The Haven	9	Wiseman's Farm
2	Delft Cottage	10	The Rhydd
3	The Firs (Greendoors)	11	Lilacs
4	Glengarry	12	Coopers
5	Holly Trees	13	Thatch Cottage
6	Vine Cottage	14	Hawthorns
7	Quiet Corner	15	Stanway Green Cottage
8	The Nook	16	Cherrytree Cottage

Several of the existing buildings in the vicinity of the Green date from Victorian times and some are considerably older. The earliest were erected by copyholders around the edges of heath before the enclosure.

I will present here a little of what I have been able to discover about each of the buildings that existed in the vicinity of the Green during the Victorian era.

The only surfaced road to the Green, formally Butchers Green, is Heath Road, formerly Butchers Lane. In Victorian times the first dwelling along here would have been a timber-framed structure known as *The Haven*. This dates back to the early 1700s and for much of its history it was divided into three dwellings and had associated with it about ½ acre (0.2 ha) of land and often an adjoining field

Left: The Haven before renovation during the 1990s. Right: The Haven. 2022

Christina Edwards

of a similar size. By 1901 it had become a single dwelling and was occupied by James Cole, a market gardener. It survived virtually unaltered until the 1960s when its first extension was added. By the 1990s the original house had become somewhat dilapidated and unstable. This was due largely to its age and lack of foundations. The problems were solved by dismantling the timber frame and completely rebuilding it in the same style. Since then the property has been altered and extended almost beyond recognition; only the profile of the earlier mansard roof provides an indication of the size of the former building.

Almost opposite *The Haven* stands *Delft Cottage*. This cottage was erected by the Copford builder, Edward Cobb, sometime between 1817 and 1838. It was built in the corner of a ¾ acre (0.3 ha) field, which along with the cottage, remained in the ownership of the Cobb family for several generations. It never appears to have been a smallholding, the land being either cultivated by the farmer of the adjoining field or used as allotments. The housing development that now covers the whole plot started during the 1930s.

Delft Cottage. 2022

Back on the other side of the road is a house that now bears the name *Greendoors*, formally *Evergreen*, originally *The Firs*. This name is now taken by a more recent house built on the land that once belonged to the original house. The house was another built by the Copford builder, Edward Cobb, sometime between 1817 and 1838. Although for many years it was rented as two dwellings, it is now one.

A little further along the road, by the postbox, is an unmade lane off to the left. A short distance along this lane that used to run alongside the northern edge of the Green, stand a pair of semidetached, late Victorian, two-bedroom cottages. The original dwellings still stand but

Greendoors. 2022

have all but disappeared hidden between more recent alterations and extensions. They now carry the names *Glengarry* and *Holly Trees*.

Back on Heath Road opposite the postbox is another unmade track, which runs beside the western edge of the Green. Along here is a building that started as a single dwelling, became two and eventually three. During the 1850s and 60s part of the premises was used as a shop by Joseph King, a Copford born farmer and dealer. Later, during the 1880s it was owned by Edward Ponder, the proprietor of the nearby Beerhouse. He bought an adjoining sliver of land where he built a small single-storey cottage called *The Nook*. During the 1950s

Glengarry and Holly Trees. 2022

Vine Cottage and Quiet Corner. 2022

the central cottage was divided between the ones either side and one of them purchased *The Nook*, which became an outbuilding that today stands in ruins.

The track leads to the southern edge of the Green where there are several ancient dwellings. *Wiseman's Farm* was discussed in the previous chapter (page 52) Tucked away near this is *The Rhydd*. The history of this building is uncertain. Some of the surviving documentary evidence appears to be contradictory. One interpretation is that the main structure of the existing building dates from shortly after 1843 and replaces an earlier building that had existed on a nearby site. Another is that the building dates back to 1770.

The Nook. 2022

It is my opinion that there could be some truth in both. The mansard roof very likely dates from the earlier date both in style and the manner in which its timbers are fashioned. When Richard Ponder purchased the land in 1843 there could have been significant remnants of the earlier cottage; even if this amounted to only what appeared to be a pile of firewood, an experienced carpenter would recognize the structure they once formed and could well have reused some or all of the timbers in the new structure. It is interesting to note that Richard always described himself as a carpenter as did his son Edward who also became the brewer at the Beerhouse.

When the present owners took possession of the property in the 1960s the basic structure of the mansard roof, which displayed many of the characteristics of an 18th century structure was still in tact although the roof covering had been partially replaced with corrugated iron and slates. It has since been sympathetically restored and extended, preserving many original features.

The Rhydd, the dormer windows of early mansard roofs often had a single pitch roof that was a continuation of the upper slope of the mansard. The original roof of this cottage had single windows of this style to both front and back.

Between *The Rhydd* and the edge of the Green sits *Lilacs*. In Victorian times this was a cottage, another built by Richard Ponder, and was often occupied by two families. In 1999 it was purchased by a developer who replaced it with the more interesting but much larger dwelling that still stands on the southern edge of the Green.

The Rhydd, its roof to the rear has been raised to cover a ground floor extension but the mansard characteristic at the front has been preserved.

The new Lilacs. 2023

Next on the Green is *Cooper's*. The existing redbrick house was built shortly after 1907. During earlier times the site was occupied by a cottage which had been called variously, *Pottey's, Champion's* and *Cooper's*, after previous owners. Throughout Victorian times it was always *Cooper's*. Thought to be named after John Cooper who, in 1705 for one reason or another, fell upon hard times resulting in him being forced to surrender his copyhold until he had reimbursed the Parish the expenses they had incurred caring for his family. It appears he failed to do this as succeeding tenants continued to pay the Parish until at least 1763. By this time the copyhold had been granted to John Ponder. The cottage remained with the Ponder family throughout most of the Victorian era.

Christina Edwards

Above: The Victorian Lilacs was demolished in 1999.

Below: Coopers. c2010

Christina Edwards

Next is *Thatch Cottage*. Although this dwelling along with its neighbour *Hawthorns* retain a certain rural charm they have been much altered and enlarged during the 20th century. It is unclear how separate these two properties were during the Victorian era. The earliest evidence of any building on this site is from a 1778 document that refers to 'a cottage that had been lately erected'. This could refer to either dwelling but most likely to *Hawthorns* as it would have been unusual at this date to build a single storey dwelling, and there were several other 1½ storey dwellings of similar design in the vicinity. There is no record of a second dwelling being erected on the site and, although during

Thatch Cottage & Hawthorns. Early 20th century

Stanway Green, Colchester.

much of the Victorian era there appear to be two families living in the property, this in itself does not imply separate buildings. What little evidence there is tends to indicate that *Thatch Cottage* evolved from an outbuilding or extension of *Hawthorns*.

As can be seen from the photographs, *Hawthorns* was a timber-framed structure with a mansard roof. The original cottage had a central chimney and no dormers on the north facing side. The three bonnet dormers were added when other alterations were made around the middle of the 20th century.

Thatch Cottage & Hawthorns. Note the presence of the winding gear frame above the well in front of Thatch Cottage. This was one of five wells in Stanway Green shown on the 1870 OS map. 2022

Stanway Green Cottage. 2022

During Victorian times there existed a pair of cottages on a small plot of land near where the lane around the Green divides into two bridleways. These were built in 1848 by the carpenter, Thomas Hutton of Birch, and were still generating rents for their owner some 50 years later. Whether or not the existing four-bedroom house that stands on the same site contains any remnant of the earlier building is difficult to tell.

The last building I am going to visit on the Green is back at the postbox. Here, set well back from the road, stand a pair of timber-framed, white weatherboard cottages under a slate roof. They are

Cherrytree Cottage, otherwise known as Ponder's Beerhouse. 2022

Grade II listed and look very much as they did when first built in 1849. They were probably erected by Edward Cobb who specialized in erecting timber-framed dwellings with slate roofs.

By 1863 the property was owned by retired farmer Robert Hunt, formally of *Lamberts Farm* (page 39) and was lived in by his daughter Maria and her husband, Edward Ponder. Edward the carpenter was also a brewer, and he operated the property as a Beerhouse, which was known as *Ponder's Beerhouse*.

The Government of the 1820s and 1830s were keen to promote beer drinking instead of spirits, especially gin. The widespread drunkenness through gin consumption was believed to be detrimental to the working class, which had led to the rise of the Temperance Society that campaigned against the easy availability of gin. The former drink of the workingman was beer but this was taxed which meant the cost of beer was too expensive for the working classes. The result of this was the passing of the Beer Act in 1830. This abolished the beer tax and extended the opening hours for premises which sold beer, but not spirits or wine. Within a few months thousands of beerhouse excise licenses were granted. Some beerhouses provided not only beer, but food, games and some lodging. There is no evidence that *Ponder's Beerhouse* ever provided these extra facilities but it must have been a successful venture as Edward continued to operate it until he died, age 84 in 1901.

Shortly after this the cottages were divided and rented out as two lets. The southern cottage remains more or less as it was when it was built.

There exist three routes from the Green to the cluster of dwellings at Bottle End. The most northerly is along Dugard Avenue; the most direct was across the fields, now through Westlands estate to Straight Road; and the most southerly is along the most ancient route to *Brickwall Farm*. I will take up the story from *Brickwall Farm*.

Until the end of Victoria's reign there were two dwellings on the Maldon Road between *Brickwall Farm* and the parish boundary and two more in the other direction between *Brickwall Farm* and the church of All Saints.

The two towards the parish boundary were *Well House Farm*, described earlier (page 82) and associated *Draw Well cottage*, a farm workers dwelling.

In the other direction stood the vicarage and a thatched single storey cottage, neither exists today. The vicarage was built in 1847 and was occupied by the first incumbent, the Reverend J S Dolby until 1864. The second incumbent, the Reverend David Hunter, enlarged the building and this was occupied by successive incumbents until 1973. The large old vicarage along with most of its ¾ acre (0.3 ha) plot

The last of the single storey thatched cottages.

Bernard Polley

was then sold and a much smaller vicarage built nearer to the church. The old vicarage site has since been developed into *Vicarage Court*, a complex of one and two bedroom apartments. Opposite the grand old Victorian vicarage stood a much more humble dwelling known as *Polley's Cottage*.

Throughout the hundreds of years when the area was a farming community the majority of workers lived in single storey dwellings just like the *Polley's Cottage*. These were not built to last and were constructed from readily available local materials. Timber for the frame, wood and clay for infilling, maybe with a weatherboard covering all under a straw roof. All fit for purpose and all biodegradable.

The *Polley's Cottage* was the last of these cottages. Due to their temporary nature they were seldom recorded and even detailed manor and estate maps often failed to indicate their existence. Those that did survive into the 20th century were often demolished or condemned by local authorities as unfit for human habitation. As has been seen at the Green a few of the more substantial dwellings from pre-Victorian times have survived and this also applies to Bottle End and Shrub End.

The first building that we come to which has survived, although much altered is the *Leather Bottle*. This public house stands on the corner of Straight Road and Shrub End Road. It is an ancient building that gave its name to the cluster of dwellings that grew up around it. The address given by the inhabitants of this part of Shrub End was

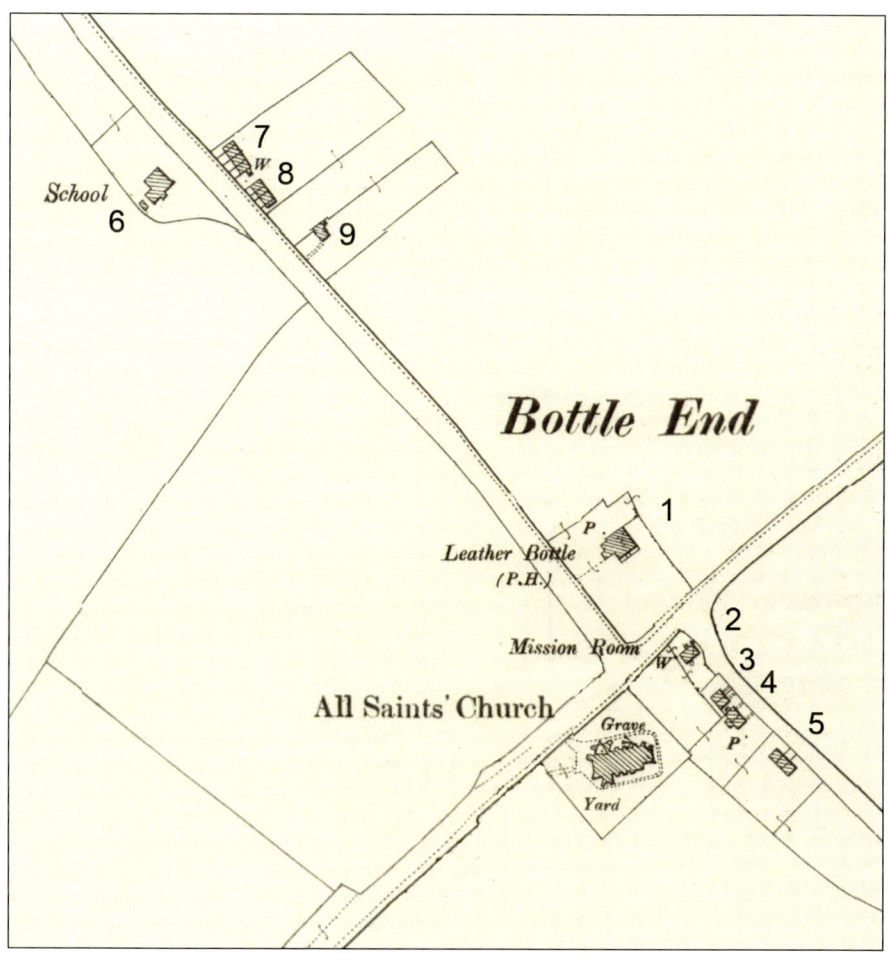

The surviving buildings that existed in Bottle End during Victorian times.

1. *Leather Bottle*   4. *10,12 Gosbecks Rd*   7. *314,316,318,320 Straight Rd*
2. *Church Cottage*   5. *16,18,20 Gosbecks Rd* 8. *322,324,326,328 Straight Rd*
3. *6,8 Gosbecks Rd* 6. *Straight Rd School*   9. *332 Straight Rd*

invariably given as Bottle End. The field opposite the pub, now the site of Gosbecks School was called Bottle field when it belonged to *Walnut Tree Farm*.

Although the building appears to have an ancient façade this is the result of several quite tasteful additions made around the turn of the 19th century. The original building was a simple rectangular structure under a mansard roof. This roof can still be seen from the car park and indicates the size of the original structure that dates from the time when this style of roof became popular in this area.

The earliest records of the property are from 1687 and by 1694 it is referred to as '*a tenement called the leather bottle*' for the first time. There is no indication that at this time it was an inn. A few years later the property was being called the '*Bottle House*' and sublet to three labouring families. It was not until the lease was held by Joseph Michael Baines from 1787 to 1819 that documentation appears indicating it, or part of it was an Inn.

It is uncertain how the pub got its name. Jess Jephcott in his *Inns, Taverns and Pubs of Colchester* suggests the Bottle house may have been used by a bottle making business. Another explanation of the name, which could also be applied to several other pubs around the country that display the Leather Bottle name, is that before the use of glass bottles became popular leather bottles were commonly used for the transport of liquids and a leather bottle was hung outside particular dwellings as a sign to indicate the availability of ale or wine. I have been unable to find any evidence to support or refute either suggestion.

Bernard Polley

The Leather Bottle when owned by Nicholl & Co Ltd. The mansard roof is just perceptible with its three dormers behind the ground floor extensions. c1900

The Leather Bottle after the 1st floor extensions had been added. 1930s

Bernard Polley

The Leather Bottle. 2023

The *Leather Bottle* at Bottle End is shown in the alehouse recognizances from 1811 and the census records provide information about occupants' names and how they styled themselves.

1841	William Smith	age 45	innkeeper
1851	William Smith	62	innkeeper
1861	William Smith	72	licensed victualler
1871	Henry Wade	38	publican
1881	Henry Wade	48	innkeeper
1891	Lavinia E Roofe	35	publican
1901	Henry Martin	40	publican
1911	James Winsborough	54	publican

William Smith appears to have had some difficulty in recalling his age but there is no doubt he was the innkeeper for over thirty years. He was succeeded by Henry Wade who had married William's youngest daughter Rhoda when she was nineteen in 1856. After William's death Henry and Rhoda continued to run the pub into the 1880s. The next recorded publican was Lavinia Roofe, a Brightlingsea girl who was the wife of Colchester-born Walter Roofe of independent means. They were both resident at the *Leather Bottle* at the time of the 1891 census. Neither of the two publicans who followed Lavinia were local; I suspect from the birthplaces of their children they had had a life in the army before settling in Colchester.

Before leaving the *Leather Bottle* I will go back to 1841 when an additional resident with the nine members of the Smith family was the blacksmith, John Tampion. During the 19th century it was not uncommon for wayside inns to offer travellers the services of a smith.

Smithy working at Shrub End Forge. 1930s

Bernard Polley

The origins of the blacksmiths' shop at Bottle End are uncertain. In 1745 the copyhold of what was to become *Church Cottage* was held by Benjamin Nuttman, a blacksmith of Chappel, who held other land in Birch and Stanway. At that time the cottage was described as brick-built standing in twenty poles (500 square metres) of land on the waste near the *Leather Bottle*. The cottage was split into two dwellings and let to two tenants. Upon the death of Benjamin in 1759 the cottage passed to his son, also Benjamin and also a blacksmith. He bought the freehold of the property from the Manor of Stanway in 1791.

Despite the fact that both Benjamin Nuttmans were blacksmiths and the cottage back garden became the site of the forge, there is no documented evidence of a blacksmiths' shop operating at the site at any time between 1740 and 1840.

The first time a blacksmiths' shop is documented was not until 1884 when the blacksmiths' forge in Gosbecks Road was recorded as being owned by Mrs Tampion. The Tampion family had a forge in Copford and were known to the Smiths at the *Leather Bottle*. John Tampion was resident at the pub in 1841 and gave his occupation as blacksmith. It is possible that he was operating a forge in one of the pub's outbuildings until the family bought the cottage opposite, where they established the Gosbecks Road forge and installed Simon Bullock, who was the son-in-law of the Stanway blacksmith, Samuel Bright, to operate it.

By 1891 the tenant was George Drane who retired sometime before 1901 to live in Colchester with his daughter and her family. The forge was then operated by William James for a short while before being worked by the Tampion family themselves until around 1912.

The last blacksmith to work the forge was the 25 year-old Horace Galley who had served his apprenticeship at Marks Tey. The business does not appear to have been prospering and in 1918 it was advertised for sale with vacant possession. The purchaser was the acquisitive George Blake who was at that time farming Magazine Farm amongst other places.

How long the premises traded after this is unclear but in 1928, consent was granted to change the blacksmiths' workshop into the double cottage that now stands on the site as 2 and 4 Gosbecks Road.

No more than a ¼ mile along Shrub End Road in the Colchester direction is another public house, *The Berechurch Arms*. This too, has a long history first appearing in trade directories as early as 1832. Before adopting the name of *The Berechurch Arms* it was known as the *Round House*. Although never round, the original building was octagonal, the shape and size of which can be deduced from the roof that can be seen from the car park.

Rear view of the Berechurch Arms showing the old Round House. 2023

Berechurch Arms. 1960

Berechurch Arms. 2022

The octagonal building along with its name appears on the tithe map of 1838. At that time the owner of the premises was Francis Smythies and the innkeeper was Temperance Biggs. A somewhat incongruous name considering her chosen occupation, which her parents could not have imagined when she was baptized. Temperance was still the recorded innkeeper at the age of 80 in 1851. Living with her was her widowed daughter, Elizabeth Norfolk, who took over when her mother died in 1853. At about this time the establishment was bought by Daniells Brewery who kept on Elizabeth who by 1861 was described as a 58 year-old licensed victualer. Unfortunately she was not as long lived as her mother and died at the age of 68. However, the running of *The Berechurch Arms* remained in the family with the job going to Elizabeth's niece, Susannah Eagle. In 1871 Susannah was recorded as a 20 year-old, unmarried victualler; a young person to be running a pub. It wasn't long before she married John Sutton at All Saints', Shrub End in January 1872.

After so many years of stability, there followed many years of changes of ownership and occupants. In 1876 the premises were sold to Nichols, then in 1884 back to Daniells Brewery. The occupants appear to have changed frequently until 1900 when the brewery invested in revamping the premises and Emma Jane Wade took over the running of the establishment. Her name appears regularly in Kelly's directories until 1912 when there was another change of ownership and Trumans took over.

In 1985 *The Berechurch Arms* was bought by Huntsman Taverns who extended it, carried out an extensive refurbishment and changed its name to their brand name. This it retained until it was bought by a new owner in 2012 who performed another refurbishment and returned it to its former name.

Francis Smythies who owned the copyhold of *The Berechurch Arms* also held the adjoining plot on which stood the windmill. This would have been the most conspicuous mill in the village, but this was not the only mill operating at this time. There was also a steam-powered mill operating in a building in Gosbecks Road close to the *Leather Bottle* crossroads. However both of these mills were preceded by many years by a water mill on Roman River at the southern extremity of the parish.

When the new parish of Shrub End was created as the parish of Stanway All Saints' in 1845 its southern boundary was extended by over 700 acres (280 ha) of uninhabited farmland so as to include the isolated *Baymill cottages*. These were the last vestiges of the former Bay Mill, which stood close by, on the river.

The Chapman & André 1777 map shows two mills, one on Roman River and the other on Birch Brook, no more than a ¼ mile apart. Hervey Benham refers to the one on Roman River as the Stanway Mill and other as the Birch Mill. The modern OS map conveniently prints 'Baymill' between the two sites. The Domesday records indicate that Stanway had three mills, so it seems likely that one of these was the Stanway Mill. If the Birch Mill stood on the site of the mill mentioned

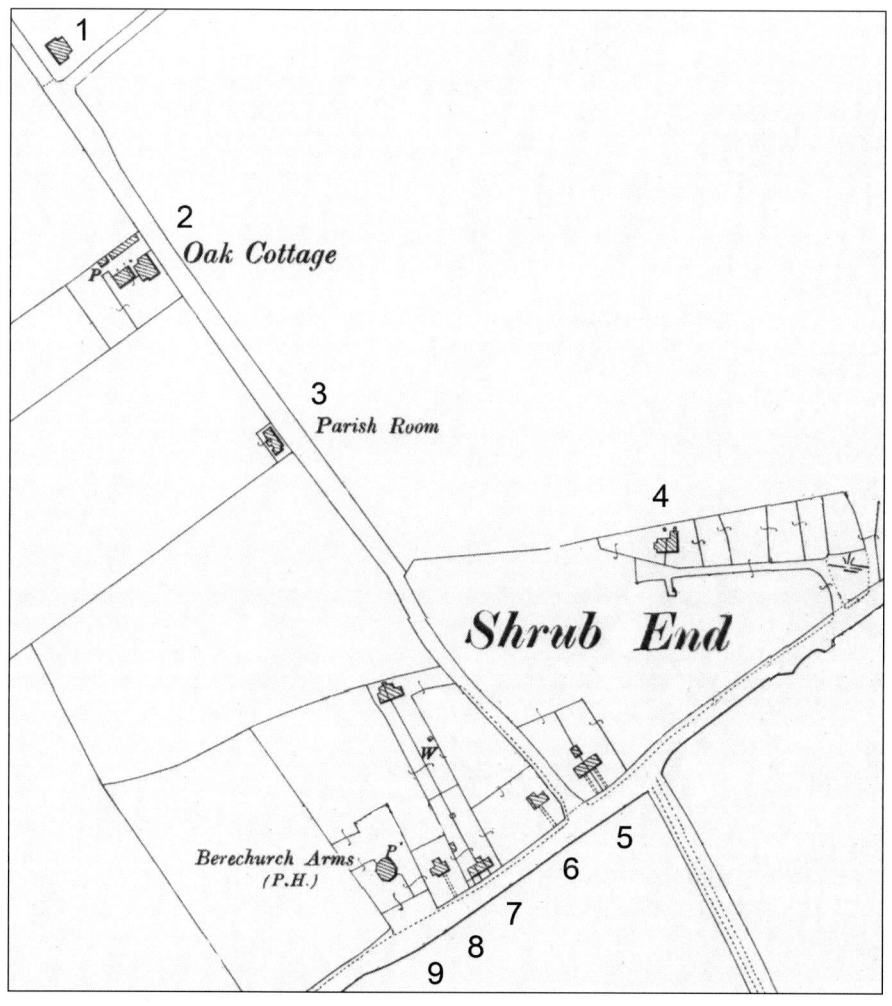

The surviving buildings that existed in Shrub End during Victorian times.

1. High Chimneys   4. Little Timbers   7. 169,171,173 Shrub End Rd
2. The Oaks   5. 157, 159 Shrub End Rd 8. 175 Shrub End Rd
3. The Life House   6. 161 Shrub End Rd   9. Berechurch Arms

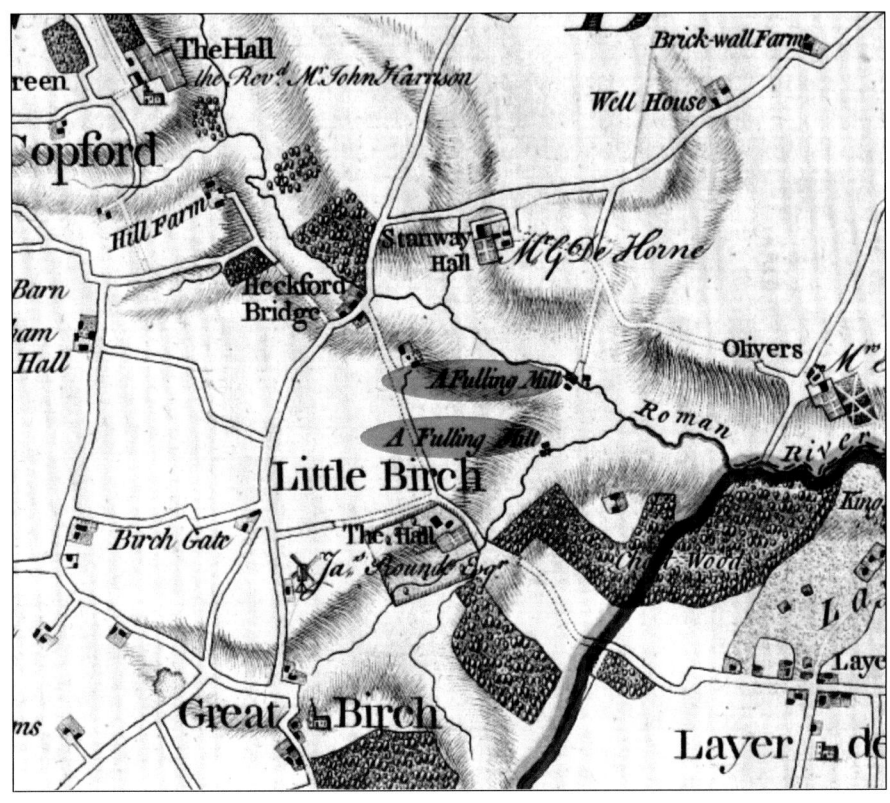

The 1777 Chapman & André map shows a Fulling Mill on Roman River. The location of this is within the parish of Shrub End.

in the Domesday Book then both of these sites have been used for milling since Saxon times. During those early times the mills would have been used as corn mills and would not have changed to fulling until it was economical to do so.

The close-by town of Colchester had long been associated with the cloth industry. There are records of cloth being made in Colchester from shortly after the Norman Conquest and the industry soon became established as a major activity in the town. From as early as 1346, Colchester cloth was being exported from the town's port to France. Also, by this time, there were at least eight mills in the town, some of which were involved in the industry. Then, with the arrival of the Dutch refugees and the introduction of Bay and Say making, the industry expanded even more. The quality of these new draperies was such that Colchester cloth appealed to markets all over Europe.

At this time many country mills of the town's hinterland took advantage of the opportunities offered by the cloth trade. Colchester Bay was a light woollen fabric that soon became the favoured material for many items of clothing including shirts and petticoats. It was soon referred to as 'bays' that evolved into 'baize'. Colchester Say was much thicker and was used for monks' habits and the coarse shirts and aprons worn by Quakers. The relatively small flow of Roman River made the

The existing bridle way runs through the middle of the vanished Roman River mill complex over a modern bridge

Baymill Cottages, Superior Victorian (c1840) farm workers dwellings.

Geoff Pettit

lighter bay cloth the more suitable to be processed at the Stanway site, hence its name *Baymill*.

Surviving records indicate the Stanway Mill was variously known as the Fulling Mill, Bay Mill, Bays Mill or Cooper's Mill, after one of the owners. By the late 18th century the cloth trade was in serious decline. The last person known to have worked the Stanway mill was Edward Kent, bay miller, who left the mill in 1801. Many of the redundant fulling mills reverted to milling corn. Unfortunately this was not an option for the Stanway/Birch mills as the valley had become depopulated. Both mills are shown on first edition OS map of 1805 but, by the time of the 1893 revision, both had disappeared. The mill and millhouse may have been used to provide accommodation for workers on Stanway Hall Farm on whose land they stood but, when the buildings became uneconomic to repair, they were replaced by a smart new pair of cottages up the hill from the old mill site.

It is known these were built c1840 and were later described as superior brick and tile cottages each with three bedrooms all with fireplaces. They were inhabited until the 1960s, since when they became ruinous and have now completely disappeared.

Shrub End windmill stood back from Shrub End Road close to *The Berechurch Arms*. Before the parish of Shrub End was formed, this was in the parish of Lexden whose Lord of the Manor was John Papillon. In 1820 he purchased a windmill for £800 and transported it from its previous home in Magdalen Street to Shrub End. There are reports from this time of windmills being transported as complete structures but there are no such accounts concerning Shrub End mill. In fact there is considerable evidence to suggest that the mill was dismantled for transportation and re-erection. At about this time Lexden had lost one of its mills that stood close to Colchester and no doubt Papillon thought a more suitable location for a new mill would be on the high ground of Lexden Heath which at that time was yet to be enclosed.

There are no surviving images of the mill but it is likely to have been similar to other contemporary post mills in the area. It was, without doubt, a post mill as its roundhouse survived until 1972. When the mill body had been removed, probably during the 1870s, the roundhouse roof aperture was tiled over leaving the internal substructure intact. When this was examined after the demolition of 1972 it was revealed the timbers had new joints cut into them so as to provide a larger diameter base than that of the earlier structure. Their dimensions and those of the main post provide enough information to estimate the size of the mill. The main post was cut from 28-inch (70 cm) square heart of oak. This supported the whole weight of the mill and provided the pivot about which it could be rotated so as to face into the wind.

It is known to have been capable of driving two pairs of stones and operated for about fifty years from shortly after erection in 1820.

The Steam mill, although the most modern to exist in the parish was the shortest lived as it worked a mere ten years or so from around 1857. It was located behind what is now 10 and 12 Gosbecks Road.

This pair of three-storey brick cottages were originally erected in 1817 by Joseph Michael Baines. They were soon extended and made into one large building, which in 1868 consisted of a parlour, keeping room, small parlour, kitchen, bake-office with large oven, pantry, storeroom and six bedrooms. The outbuildings included a coach house and stable along with a brick and slated mill-house with a workshop.

The mill stood back from the present frontage and had a large orchard in front of it. Access to the mill was along the lane that has now disappeared but at that time ran from further along Gosbecks Road, behind the cottages that then existed, through what is now part of the churchyard to join Shrub End Road opposite Straight Road.

The earliest record of the steam mill dates from 1857 when it was held by Timothy Wagstaff who also held the windmill in Shrub End Road. By 1861 the mill had changed ownership but was still being operated by Timothy Wagstaff.

Left: Shrub End mill roundhouse nearly a century after the mill's last recorded use. Note the mill stones by the door. 1972

Right: A drawing of how the Shrub End Mill could have looked during its working years 1820 - 1870.

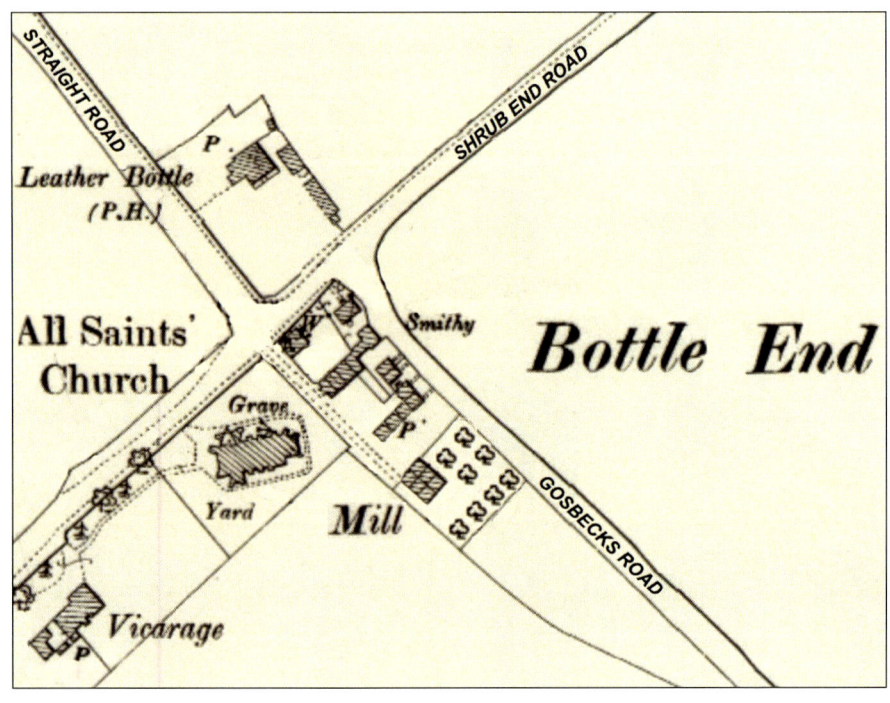

Map of Bottle End c1870 when the steam mill was in operation.
(compiled from contemporary information)

When the mill was sold it was not a going concern but there was an option to buy the 'steam-engine, boiler, mill-stones, going gears and apparatus in the mill house'. It is highly likely this option was taken up by the purchasers as the tenants of both mills were Albert J Merry and George E Merry; both were millers and each were employing an additional miller in 1871. This, however, was to be a short-lived venture as the Merrys became bankrupt later that year. I have been unable to find any further records concerning either mill.

Before mentioning the few surviving Victorian and earlier private dwellings in Shrub End I will present some of what I have been able to discover concerning a building that played an important part in the life of the Victorian community, the school.

The first reference to this school dates from 1860 when a Deed of Gift was made by the High Sheriff of Essex, Mr G H Errington, who lived at Lexden Park, to the Minister and Church Wardens of the Ecclesiastical District of All Saints', 'for the erection of a School and School House thereon for the education of poor persons of and in the parish'. The small plot of land is believed to have been used as a gravel pit to provide material for road and path making at Lexden Park.

The architect of the school was Mr H W Hayward and the All Saints' National School was built in Straight Road at a cost of £350 and opened in March 1861. The first schoolmistress was Miss Mary Hawkins who had 70 infant pupils in her care. At this time there was just one schoolroom, which was extended in 1882, to be followed in 1910 by the addition of a second classroom to cope with the increasing number of pupils.

By 1876 the headteacher was Mr Charles Grimwood who was to serve the school for some 35 years. For most of these he would take the whole school to *Kingsford Park*, the home for many years of the Egerton-Green family, for the school's annual summer party. This was kindly provided by Mrs Egerton-Green who not only provided the venue for various games and amusements, but also a

Bernard Polley

All Saints' National School. 1915

All Saints' School building. 2023

bountiful tea. The event also provided an opportunity for the singing of songs and the presentation of prizes.

One of the 'poor persons of and in the parish' was Lilian Carter, the eldest of seven children who lived at *Baymill cottages*. She related some of her memories to Geoff Pettit. The cottages had no water, gas or electricity, they collected drinking water from a nearby spring, used oil lamps for lighting and wood for fires and the kitchen range for cooking. It was a long walk to school along tracks and footpaths that seemed even longer in the winter mud. Despite all this Lilian said she had a very happy childhood and loved playing in the fields and woods.

The school catered for mixed and infants until 1930 when children over 11 year-old were transferred to the new Lexden School, and the school changed its name to Shrub End Junior Mixed and Infants.

By the 1920s the school was accommodating 108 pupils, with headmaster Mr Millington living in the adjoining house. The school closed in 1970 with existing staff and pupils being transferred to Lexden School. Since closure, the school has had many uses including as an adult education centre, youth club, pre-school and polling station.

Some of the first children attending this school could well have lived in the surviving pre-Victorian and Victorian buildings not mentioned elsewhere. These include over twenty brick-built cottages, a single surviving white weatherboard dwelling and four buildings each under a mansard roof.

Bernard Polley

Straight Road looking towards the church from outside the school with its wooden palings on the right. The two rows of Victorian cottages on the left still stand today.

The surviving Victorian terraces in Straight Road. 2023

In addition to the brick-built cottages opposite the school there are other survivors in Shrub End Road and Gosbecks Road;

Top: A much-extended detached Victorian cottage at 175 Shrub End Road. 2022

Middle: A terrace of three Victorian cottages at 169/171/173 Shrub End Road. 2022

Below: This 1930s postcard of Shrub End Road looking towards Colchester shows the entrance to the Berechurch Arms on the left. Beyond this is the Victorian detached no175 and a sideview of the Victorian terrace, nos 169-173.

A pair of extended semidetached Victorian cottages at 157/159 Shrub End Road.
The white extension on the right is on the site of Allen's lean-to shop. 2022

Apart from the brick-built cottages, there is one timber-framed cottage that has survived from an earlier era. Similar in date and construction to *Cherrytree Cottage* at Stanway Green, the house on the corner of King Harold Road, 161 Shrub End Road has just about survived. This building began to loose some of its traditional features during the early years of the 21st century when its white weatherboard front was rendered over. From then on the building underwent piecemeal modernization followed by a period of neglect before falling into disrepair and the threat of demolition. Fortunately this did not happen and the cottage has now been restored sympathetically.

The building acquired local listed status in 2020. This describes it as an early 19th century example of modest late Georgian vernacular weatherboard architecture. Although the building has been altered

A pair of much altered semidetached Victorian cottages at 6/8 Gosbecks Road. Only the slate roof and central chimney stack are original features. 2022

A pair of semidetached Victorian cottages at 10/12 Gosbecks Road (The High House). The appearance of this building has changed many times over the years. 2022

A terrace of three Victorian cottages at 16/18/20 Gosbecks Road. All have been extended and had front porches added. Only no 18 retains windows of a similar size and shape as the originals. 2022

several times and was extensively refurbished in 2022 it remains an interesting example of a small workers cottage, once common on the Essex heaths.

Left: 161 Shrub End Road, although the front was rendered during the early years of the 21st century, this is the only remaining pre-Victorian weatherboard cottage in Shrub End Road.

Below: The sympathetically restored 161 Shrub End Road, on the corner with King Harold Road. 2023

A short distance from King Harold Road is Pond Chase and along here is *Little Timbers*. The Chase is now a cul-de-sac but before the enclosure of Lexden heath this lane led past the cottage onto the heath. It is likely the timber-framed structure was built in the 17th century or earlier.

Little Timbers after restoration and its 1st extension.

Bernard Polley

Little Timbers after restoration and its 2nd extension. 2020

Left: Little Timbers before restoration and extension.

Below: An impression of how Little Timbers may have looked in the 17th century.

Bernard Polley
Lexden Morant

POND CHASE

An extract from the 1805 OS 1 inch map showing Pond Chase leading on to Lexden Heath. King Harold Road was built after enclosure along the north east edge of the heath and straight on, across the former clearing, to join Shrub End Road.

The unnamed building south of Squirrels Farm is Prettygate Farm, formerly Coopers or Cowpers Farm. To the west of this is High Chimneys.

The most westerly building on the north side of Pond Chase is in the position occupied by Little Timbers and to the east of this is the unnamed Plume Farm.

The cluster of buildings to the south of Shrub End Road include what became Walnut Tree Farm and Rayner's Farm. The cartographer appears to have interposed the names of Bottle End and Shrub End.

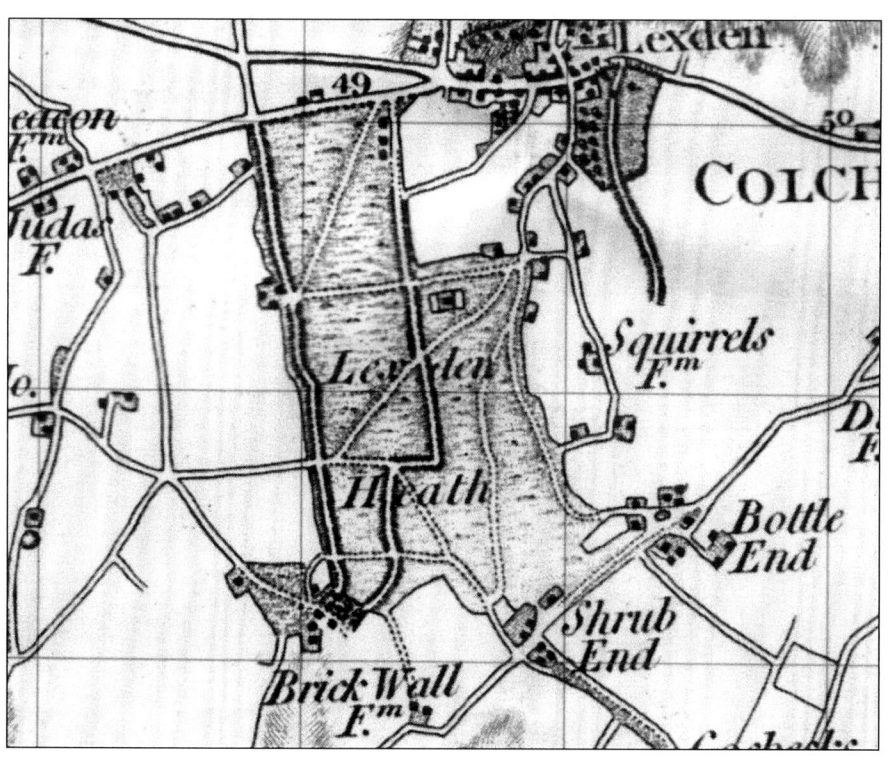

Close by this cottage were several timber-framed and weatherboard houses similar to *Cherrytree Cottage* at Stanway Green (Page 109). The last of these in Shrub End, 161 Shrub End Road, has already been mentioned. Close by this, on the land between Pond Chase and Shrub End Road, stood another similar building. During the late Victorian times this weatherboard house was lived in by Jack Woodrow who was known as Mad Jack. He ran a horse-drawn carriage/taxi and did not hang about. One customer who complained about the rough ride he had experienced to Mersea told Jack that he would not ride with him again. Jack took the shilling (5p) fare and said, 'I'll make sure you won't'.

Plum Tree Cottage. 2022

Jack's old house was demolished in 1978 to make way for Wilkin Court, a mixed sheltered accommodation development. This is accessed from King Harold Road where there is both another cottage and a house each with a mansard roof.

Plum Tree Cottage is thought to have been built in 1829. It is brick-built with corbelling at the eaves. There is a stone plaque built into the south wall, which unfortunately is no longer legible but may have shown the date and initials of the builder, which may have been 1829, H H. In 1841 one of the residents on Lexden Heath is recorded as Henry Howard, age 55, builder. On early maps the building is shown as a pair of cottages with gardens extending towards Shrub End Road.

1st Ed OS 25 inch map. Plum Tree Cottage shown in red

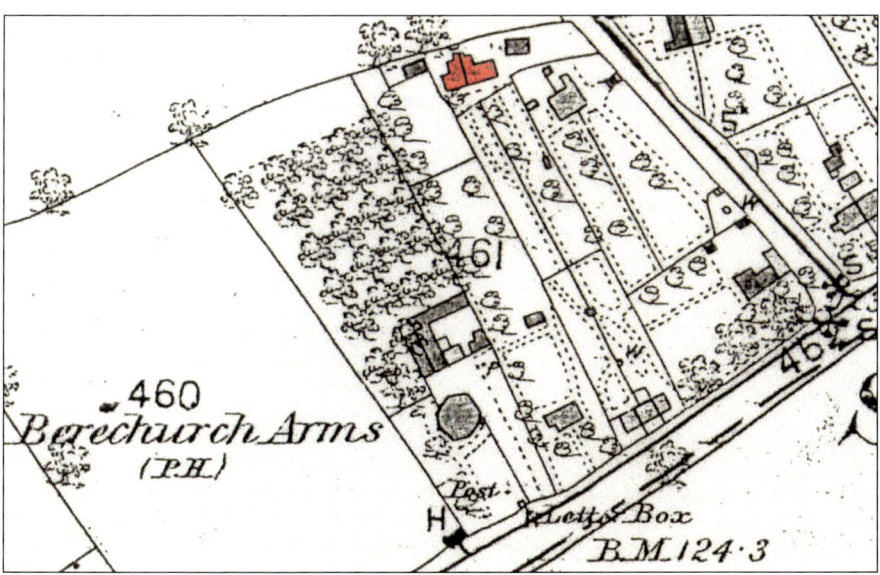

HIGH CHIMNEYS

Lexden Morant

The Oaks, apart from the renewal of the roof covering from slate to tile during the mid 20th century this Georgian style building remains remarkably unchanged since it was built c 1840.

Before leaving King Harold Road there is another Georgian/ Victorian house that deserves a mention.

The house named *The Oaks* in King Harold Road has long fascinated me. If not the oldest it is certainly the most elegant building in the road. Over the years I have spent many hours researching the history of this dwelling. The results were largely disappointing often producing only vague and ambiguous results. Recently this all changed when the present owner of the property gave me access to the house deeds. This enabled me to make sense of my collection of disparate information.

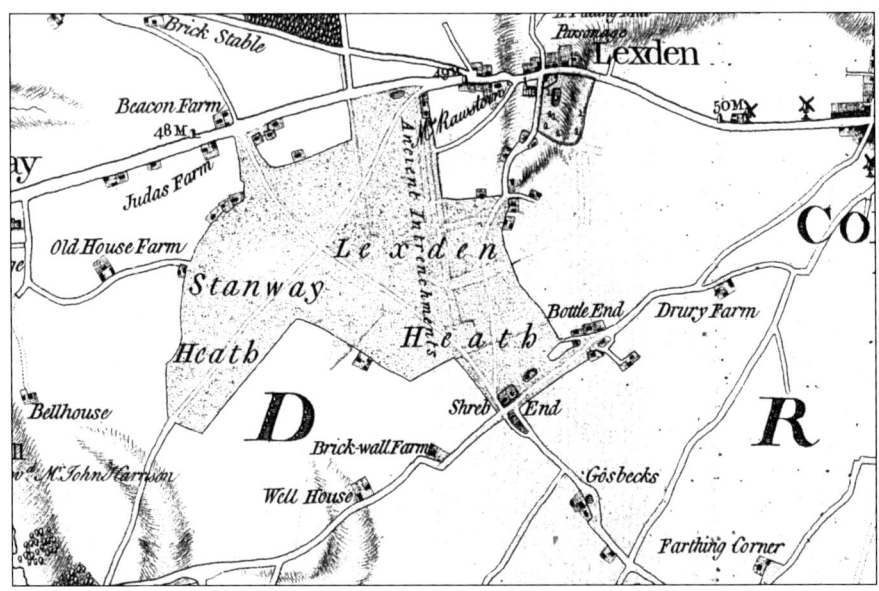

The Chapman & André map shows the extent of the heath in 1777.

The deeds date back to a time before the house was built. A time when the land on which it stands was part of Lexden Heath, which was until the Enclosure Acts of 1820 a significant area of what became the parish of Shrub End and was accessible to all.

The Commissioners of this act allocated the copyhold of the land on which *The Oaks* now stands to John Bridge. It was called Allotment 42, an area of one acre and twenty-six perches (0.46 ha). During the following ten years or so the copyhold was transferred several times until it rested in the hands of Thomas Brown, a yeoman farmer of Lexden.

A document from 1834 refers to 'a messuage or tenement and barn lately erected and built by the said Thomas Brown upon part of the said piece or parcel of land now in his own occupation'. This is the earliest reference to there being any buildings on the site. It implies these were built sometime around 1830.

This date for the earliest buildings on the site is supported by the Enclosure maps of 1821 and 1828 which both show *High Chimneys* but not *The Oaks,* and the Tithe map of 1838 which on the site of *The Oaks* shows a single dwelling set back from the road with outbuildings alongside. This map confirms the suspicions held by many that the building behind *The Oaks* referred to in early documents as *Oak Cottage* predates it. The 1841 census lists three occupants in a dwelling close by the *High House,* an earlier name of *High Chimneys* in Squirrels Lane, an earlier name of King Harold Road. The occupants of the unnamed house were; Thomas Brown, age 40, a Farmer; his wife, Elizabeth, age 40 and; Sophia Gregson, age 50 of independent means.

It could not have been long after this date that *The Oaks* was built; in fact it could have been being built in 1841, as this was the year during which the survey for the 1st edition of the large scale map OS map was conducted showing an additional building between the original dwelling and the road. If this is so then *The Oaks* was built during the early years of Queen Victoria's reign but this does not detract at all from its elegant Georgian proportion and styling.

Above: The 1838 Tithe map shows a single building set well back from the road.

Right: The earliest building on the Oaks site, now 72 King Harold Road. 1950s

Below: The 1841 OS 6 inch map shows an additional building closer to the road.

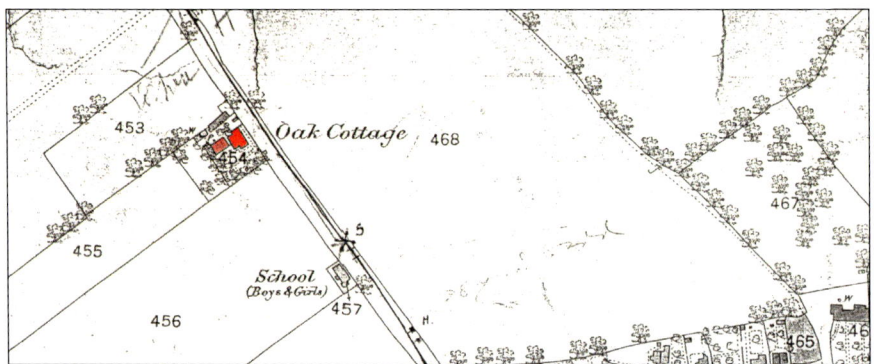

I would like to think Thomas Brown enjoyed his new house as he was to die a few years later in 1845 at the young age of 44. The property passed to his wife, Elizabeth, who later married Isaac Wenlock and the couple appear in the 1851 Census at *Oak Cottage*.

Isaac Wenlock	Head	M	48	Farmer
Elizabeth	Wife	M	50	
James Beard		W	48	Rtd Ironmonger

By 1853 the property was in the hands of yet another farmer, James Polley, who turned out to be more long-lived than earlier inhabitants of the house.

James Polley died in 1889 at the age of 97 and was buried at All Saints', Shrub End on 27th May. He left the property described as 'two freehold messuages and premises situate at Shrub End' valued at £280 to Eliza Jane Hawes.

The Hawes were obviously friends, if not related to the Polleys, and were living with them in 1871. Following her inheritance it appears Eliza lived alone in the property with a couple of servants until her death in 1897 when she too was buried at All Saints', Shrub End. Her estate passed into the hands of her son, John Arthur Hawes, and her daughter, Catherine Jane Barleyman. It appears they derived an income from the Shrub End property by letting it to tenants.

These proved to be of a varied nature. In 1901 the house was occupied by a young Clergyman of the Church of England, Noel

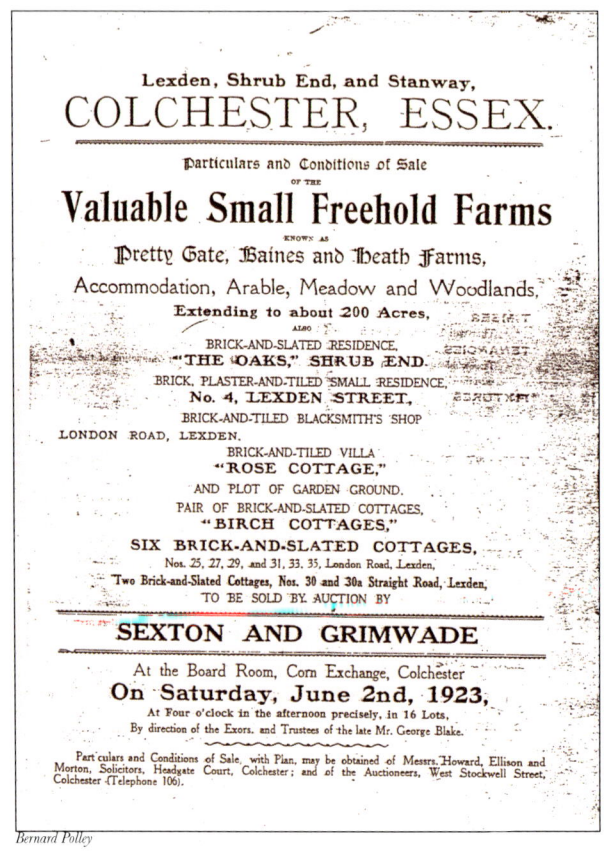

A page from the Auction Catalogue disposing of the assets of the Lexden Manor Estate in 1923, which describes The Oaks as a 'Brick, plaster and tiled small residence'

Johnson, with his wife, Kathlene, and their baby daughter Minnie who were all being helped by his Sister-in-Law plus a single servant.

Ten years later the property was, for the first time, referred to as *The Oaks* and was occupied by Ellen Mary Born, a 60 year-old widow of private means and Albert George Gammer, an unmarried 27 year-old who described himself as a lodger and farmer. It is likely but uncertain that Ellen Mary's only child, Irene Nellie Jane, was also a resident of *The Oaks* but on the day when the 1911 census was taken she is recorded as a visitor at the Gammer household at 19 Barrington Road, Colchester. The Gammers were a large family with origins in the local area but do seem to have moved around a lot.

Albert George was the fifth of ten children to a father, William John, who was variously described as a dealer, farmer and hay merchant. He may well have had more than one brush with the law but overall appeared to be successful, was able to support his family and managed to accumulate the best part of £9000 to leave to his wife at his death in 1925. His third son seems to have inherited many of his attributes and followed a similar career in farming and dealing. He too was successful in these activities and accumulated sufficient wealth to purchase *The Oaks* when it was sold in 1923. By this time it had become a freehold property, after being held for many years copyhold from Lexden Manor.

In the 1929 Kelly's Directory of Colchester, A G Gammer has two entries: one as the Resident of *The Oaks* and the other as Farmer of Drury Farm. But all was not sweetness and light as Albert was brought before the local courts on several occasions and appears to have become addicted to drink. His last court appearance resulting in him being bound over for six months as reported in the Chelmsford Chronicle on 28th May 1926.

REMARKABLE CASE AT AT COLCHESTER

At Colchester on Tuesday, Albert Geo. Gammer, hay dealer, of the Oaks, Shrub End was summoned for driving a motor car while drunk on April 30, and also for assaulting Miss Irene Nellie Jane Born, of the same address, on May 20. — Mr. O. Thompson Smith defended.

Insp. Stamp, R.S.P.C.A. living at King Harold Road, Shrub End, deposed that the defendant drove home at about 10.30 p.m. in a zig-zag manner, and was drunk, landing the car in a ditch. Upon arrest he became violent, and was handcuffed, and his legs tied up with rope.

Miss Born said the car made several attempts to get into the garage, and ultimately went back into the ditch.

Mr. O. Thompson Smith said Gammer was at the Bull Hotel that evening, and as he left he was taken queer. He asked Mr. Green, the landlord, to drive him home, and Mr. Green did so. Upon arrival at the house, Green went away. Gammer then gave the car a push to get it into the garage. He, however, gave it too much of a push, and the car ran off backwards and down into the ditch outside in the road. Gammer was never in charge of the car.

Gammer said there had been a good deal of unpleasantness through Inspector Stamp and Miss Born.

Inspector Stamp, re-called, declared that defendant was driving the car, and he never saw Green there at all.

Mr. Smith: Did you tell Mr. Lampon, jun., that you had been waiting for Gammer for twelve months, and you hoped he would get a month? — No.

The Chairman (Mr. C. M. Stanford) said that, owing to the conflicting evidence, they had reluctantly come to the conclusion that by a majority they must dismiss the case.

The summons for assault was then proceeded with.

Mr. F. J. Collinge, for Miss Born, said that defendant was the owner of the Oaks, of which Miss Born was tenant, and where defendant had been a lodger for many years. Defendant was addicted to drink, and Miss Born had been frequently assaulted. After defendant got to hear that she was to give evidence against him in the previous case he came home on May 20 in a quarrelsome mood. He first knocked down all the pictures. He had a knife in his hand, and he took hold of complainant roughly, and threatened her in various ways.

Miss Born said she had had to leave the house in her night attire to seek the protection of neighbours, and declared that Gammer had knocked her unconscious.

Gammer said Miss Born had declined to get his meals ready. He took the pictures off—four of them—to prepare for the decorators, and when he came to remove the clock she said, " No one will touch that clock except Mr. Stamp." Defendant denied the allegations of assault and threats.

The Chairman said the Bench considered that Gammer had exceeded the limits of good treatment, and that at times he had certainly lost his temper. Miss Born would have to be protected, and Gammer would be bound over for six months.

Chelmsford Chronicle, 28th May 1926.

154

This brings us to the 1930s, a decade during which *The Oaks* went through several changes. The most significant of which was the division of the property into two. Subsequently each was sold separately either as *The Oaks*, 70 King Harold Road – the newer Georgian style building, or as 72 King Harold Road – the earlier cottage building. Over the following years there were several minor boundary and access changes between the two properties. Then in 1958 the land that remained in the ownership of *The Oaks* but behind No 72 was sold to a local firm of builders leaving each property far more, but not completely, independent of each other.

The present owner has preserved many of the original features of the property including the stump of the last remaining oak tree that was a victim of the 1987 gale. In 1984 this tree had a girth of 7 feet (210 cm), which corresponds to an approximate age of 84 years. This tree grew from an acorn that fell around 1900 some 60 years after *The Oaks* was built around 1840, but well before it was first called *The Oaks* in 1910.

There are ten mansard roofs hidden away in the parish. Each has been described with the exception of *332 Straight Road*. Until 1997 this was a small cottage standing in large plot of about ¼ acre (0.1 ha). It is not shown on the 1805 OS map but appears on the 1st edition of the large scale OS map of 1841.

The parish of Lexden was relatively prosperous during Georgian times. Even so some families required parish help, often as a result of injury, childbirth or illnesses such as smallpox, typhus, diphtheria and

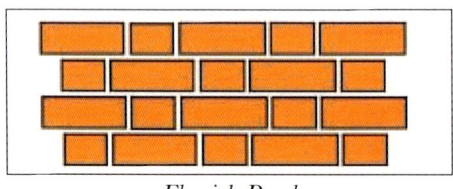

Flemish Bond

English Bond

Stretcher Bond

dysentery. It was the task of the parish overseers to decide which of the deserving parishioners would receive help. In 1823 the parish chose, for reasons that were not recorded to help Samuel Durrant build a cottage on its land at Bottle End, granting him life tenancy at a token rent. I think it was this financial help that enabled Samuel Durrant, an agricultural labourer to build *332 Straight Road*.

In 1841 the census shows Samuel living there with his wife, Margaret and their four children, the oldest of which was the 20 year-old Samuel who was described as a bricklayers apprentice. He could well have been working with his near neighbour the bricklayer, Joseph Barker who in turn could have been working for his neighbour the builder, Henry Hayward.

The cottage is brick-built under a clay-tile roof. The walls are Flemish bond with the mansard gable in stretcher bond. The Flemish bond pattern of wall construction first appeared in England during the late 17th century and was most popular during the 18th before falling out of fashion in the mid 19th.

332 Straight Road in its large garden. Pre 1997

Bernard Polley

In 1997 this 1823 cottage was extended and two bungalows were built in its garden. 2022

STRAIGHT ROAD

Lexden Morant

This appears to have been a well-built small cottage. Probably a single room with a fireplace at one end used for heating and cooking. A narrow quarter-winding stair beside the chimney would lead to a single attic room, which has a single dormer window under a roof, whose pitch follows that of the upper mansard roof.

During this period of enormous social change in England perhaps the most significant change for the people of Shrub End was the growing number of more substantial dwellings leading to higher standards of living. Materially, the villagers benefited from the increased wealth of the area from the developing building activity, the development of the forge, and the building of the mills. But spiritually and socially it was the building of village places of worship and their associated schools that was most important. For the first time the ordinary people of Shrub End had the chance of becoming literate and all the opportunities of the developing world were opened up to them.

Church Cottage, which was for many years the Egerton-Green Institute. 2023

CHAPTER 5

The Edwardian & Interwar Years

What is now called *Church Cottage* on the corner of Shrub End Road and Gosbecks Road is an ancient building. As has been mentioned previously (page 118) the date of the earliest documented evidence of a building on this site is 1745 but it could well be over 100 years older. During the renovation of the building in 1977 one of the larger timbers was dated to 1640 by dendrochronology.

Dendrochronology is the science of dating timbers by studying their annual growth rings. New cells, forming a ring, are added to the outer part of a tree trunk during each growing season. Each year's growth season in spring and summer is different resulting in differing widths of the rings. The pattern of rings from a timber of unknown age can be matched to timbers of known ages to determine its age.

The building's major significance to the village did not occur until it was acquired by Horace Egerton-Green in the early 20th century. It is very likely that it was he who gave the cottage the Victorian makeover that makes it unique among the other buildings in the parish. More significant than its mansard roof, the ornate chimney, and elaborate windows is the fact that Egerton-Green gave the refurbished building to the inhabitants of Shrub

End to be used as a reading room and meeting place for village activities. Four daily newspapers and some monthly magazines were available for readers who paid a subscription of four shillings (20p) per year. The newly literate village population had a thirst for knowledge and many benefited from the facilities offered by the Institute.

Horace Egerton-Green was a wealthy banker who lived at *Kingsford Place*, which was within the parish until the boundary changes of 1960. Horace took his social responsibilities seriously, steadfastly served his community, and was a great believer in education. He was Mayor of Colchester on two occasions, 1887 and 1897 and also served as High Sheriff of Essex. He was born in Colchester in 1838 and died in 1905. He is commemorated by a nearby road that carries his name.

Bernard Polley

Horace Egerton-Green High Sheriff of the County of Essex

Egerton-Green Road sign on the Shrub End Estate. 2022

Bernard Polley

Horace Egerton-Green Institute. 1920

The refurbished Institute bears a plaque engraved with the inscription '*At this corner stood Pedders Cross*'. At one time England was littered with wayside crosses. Some were preaching crosses, some were memorials, and others were for pilgrims indicating the route to a shrine. It is thought Pedders Cross could have been part of a Pilgrims' Way leading to Walsingham in Norfolk, known as the Pedders Way. Another possible derivation of the name is from the peddlers who would gather there to avoid paying the toll to enter Colchester to sell their wares.

The plaque built into the wall of Church Cottage. 2023

Shortly after the death of Horace Egerton-Green, his house, *Kingsford Place*, was occupied by the Digby family. Fortunately Sir Kenelm and Lady Digby shared many of the characteristics of the Egerton-Greens and continued to support the local community and take an interest in universal education. During WWI Sir Kenelm was to be responsible for the safety of all the people of Shrub End parish should the Germans land in Essex. There was a three-stage evacuation and scorched earth plan. The first was to alert the population, the second to encourage them to pack ready to leave, and the third to lead them along carefully pre-planned routes along byways out of the area. Cattle were to be killed, crops and farms to be burnt. Fortunately it was never necessary to implement this plan.

THIS PLAYGROUND IS GIVEN
FOR THE USE OF THE BOYS
AND GIRLS OF THIS PARISH
BY CAROLINE DIGBY IN
MEMORY OF HER HUSBAND
SIR KENELM DIGBY GCB
OF KINGS FORD WHO HAD
HOPED TO PROVIDE ONE
DURING HIS LIFETIME

The Digby Playground. 2023

Following the death of Sir Kenelm, his widow, Lady Digby, donated a field opposite the school in Straight Road for 'children's happiness' in his memory. It was opened by Dame Catherine Hunt in 1926.

A short distance along Shrub End Road towards Colchester, where the road narrows, stood a toll-house. What was thought to have been its foundations were discovered under the road and in the garden of 212 Shrub End Road indicating that at the time the road would have been even narrower.

By the 1920s the demand for space for social activities exceeded that which could be provided by the *Egerton-Green Institute*. The problem was solved when the Colchester businessman who owned the piece of land opposite the Institute donated it to the village. Then a sufficient number of villagers bought five-shilling (25p) shares to pay for an ex-army hut, which was erected on the site in 1924. The building, known locally as *The Hut* served the village well until 1970 when it was replaced by the purpose-built *Shrub End Social Centre*.

This well-equipped single storey building contains a large hall with a portable stage, lobby, cloakroom, kitchen, toilets, and storage area. It continues to be a thriving and appreciated asset for the local community.

Between 1900 and 1930 the number and locations of the shops and services available to the villagers altered considerably.

Bernard Polley

Above: The Hut, successor to the Egerton-Green Institute and the forerunner of Shrub End Social Centre. 1960s

Bernard Polley

Above: Shrub End Social Centre. 1970
Below: Shrub End Social Centre. 2023

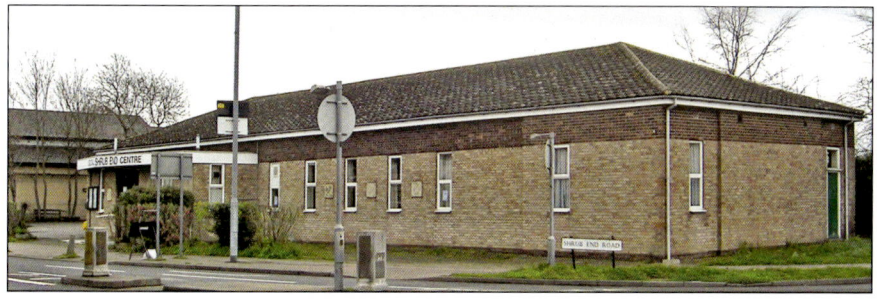

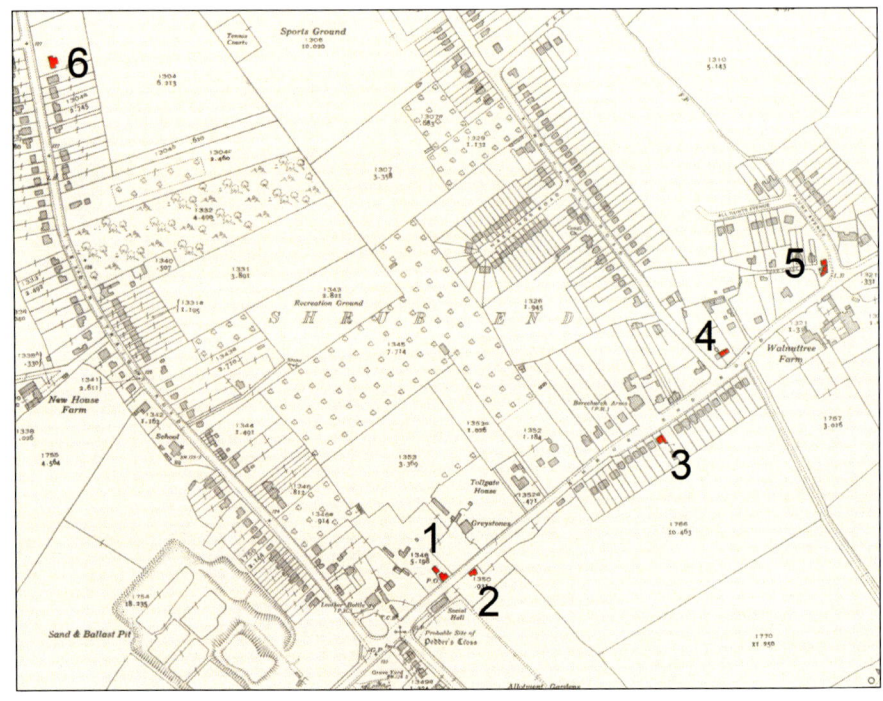

Extract from the 1939 OS map with the shops highlighted in red.

1   1st site of the PO and later general store.

2   2nd site the PO and later Magnolia Service Station.

3   3rd site of the PO and Mann's Cycle Stores.

4   Allens' general store.

5   Plume Avenue general store.

6   Williams general store.

Bernard Polley

Shrub End's first Post Office, a detached single storey building with cream-painted weatherboard exterior and tiled roof.

201 Shrub End Road. Now James & Lindsay Ltd. formerly a general store. The forecourt was the site of the original PO

At the turn of the century the village was home to essential craftsmen; blacksmith, carpenter, bricklayer, shoemaker, and had also acquired a couple of greengrocers, a pork butcher, and a Post Office soon to be joined by several general stores and a cycle store.

The original *Post Office* stood on the edge of the road in front of what is now 201 Shrub End Road, James & Lindsay Ltd., opposite the Petrol Station. It was first recorded in a directory of 1894 and was operated by Edward and Sarah Johnson. The 1901 census describes Sarah as the Postmistress and Edward as a greengrocer. By 1911 Ernest Henry Berry was the Postmaster assisted by his wife Constance Elizabeth.

169

Bernard Polley

Magnolia service station owned by Mr R W Moss and named after the Magnolia tree which stood on the site. Price of petrol was 35.2p/litre in 1986.

Bernard Polley

Magnolia service station. 2004

Magnolia filling station and Coop store. The price of petrol was 145.9p/litre in 2023

Later the Goody family ran the shop-cum-post office, first by William & Annie followed by their two daughters well into the 1930s. After this shop was demolished a replacement was built further back from the road. For many years this was opperated as a general shop by the *Woolnoughs*. It has since been the *West End Hair Salon* before being used as offices. Another shop, almost opposite, was run by Alice Morris and her daughter, Jenny. This shop was home to the *Post Office* for a while but is chiefly remembered for its cottage garden that contained a magnificent magnolia tree, which bloomed in profusion each spring. It was this tree that gave its name to the *Magnolia Service Station* and Coop Food Store that has since replaced the cottage and garden.

Meanwhile a row of new houses had been built further along Shrub End Road. One of these, number 192, was occupied by Mr E G Mann who in 1931 built a wooden extension onto the side of his house and opened *Shrub End Cycle Stores*. Here he sold new cycles as well as carrying out repairs. He charged sixpence ($2\frac{1}{2}$p) to mend a puncture and sold new cycles for less than £5.

After WWII the house and cycle business was sold to Mr Lambert who opened the *Post Office* in the front room of the house. This was to be the last move of the *Post Office*. In 2023 it was still operating from the same room although the cycle store is long gone. During the 1980s the wooden lean-to was replaced by a brick extension. This was later demolished and replaced by a separate detached dwelling. The side of the existing shop and Post Office still carries the scar of *Mr Mann's Cycle Stores*.

Bernard Polley

Mr E G Mann in the doorway of his Shrub End Cycle Stores. 1932

Bernard Polley

The extended Shrub End Post Office and shop after being acquired by Tara Traders. 1988

The new house and just the scar of Mr Mann's Cycle Stores on the side of the PO. 2023

Mr Mann's Cycle Stores was not the only lean-to shop in the village. On the opposite side of the road the Victorian semi, number 157, was for many years occupied by Mr & Mrs Allen who operated a general store from their wooden lean-to. Their store was popular with youngsters for their range of sweets and chocolates but they also carried a surprising stock of essentials. The unpretentious shop never looked open but was seldom closed. I had the impression that if one of the Allens was awake the shop was open. A very useful service for the forgetful in the days of Sunday closing and regulated opening hours.

There was also a small convenience shop in Straight Road. This was attached to the side of number 246, opposite Dugard Avenue and was run by Edgar Hazelton. Also, during the late 1930s Mr W R Williams opened a general store on the corner of Plume Avenue.

The Allen's lean-to shop altered for residential use during the late 20th century.

Bernard Polley

One of three pairs of Victorian/Edwardian semis, 24/26 Gosbecks Road.
(Note the white stone cills and lintels characteristic of this period.) 2023

During the Edwardian and post WWI period there was considerable building in the parish. Generally those houses, large or small, built during the Edwardian period were well built and most of them have survived. Among them are *Coopers*, at Stanway Green, illustrated on page 105 and three pairs of semidetached houses in Gosbecks Road.

There were two larger properties in the parish dating from this period. Close to the *Leather Bottle* on Shrub End Road stands *Greystones*. This handsome structure was built using the grey coloured gault bricks

The Victorian/Edwardian Greystones. 2022

to a Victorian-Edwardian design. It has always been known as *Greystones* but originally carried the address of No 3 Shrub End and is now 191 Shrub End Road.

For many years it was home to retired army officer Hugh Stockwell, Chief Constable of Colchester Borough Police. In 1913 working from the Police Station in the basement of the Town Hall, Captain Stockwell and his wife, Gertrude, took up residence at *Greystones*. In 1915 he was released temporarily from his civic duty to rejoin the army as Provost Marshall serving in France. On release in 1919, having been promoted to Lt Colonel, he was back home as Chief Constable. During WWII Stockwell's responsibility was to oversee all wartime restrictions imposed on civilians in the town. Stockwell retired in 1974 when Colchester Borough Police Force was merged with Essex County Police Force.

Almost next door to *Greystones* stood *Tollgate House*; built of redbrick with a slate roof, it stood well back from the road. This was the home of Brigadier General Francis Towsey and his wife, Florence. They were quite wealthy and displayed it by being driven around in a high-backed Bentley car by a uniformed chauffeur. Mrs Towsey was also a keen animal lover and each day she had a bowl of fresh water placed outside the house on the pavement for quenching the thirst of passing dogs. The house has since been demolished and its extensive grounds are now occupied by some of the houses in the Red Mill development.

Much closer to Colchester, on the parish boundary, at the corner of Shrub End Road and, what is now Norman Way, is what appears to be a fine Tudor house. This is not quite what it appears to be. It is believed to have been an old Suffolk farmhouse, which was bought by Mr Charles Leeds, a well-known Colchester butcher renowned for its excellent lamb, who had the old building reconstructed on this site in the early 1930s when this site was surrounded by farmland. Travelling along Shrub End Road from Colchester it was the first and only house in the parish until *Walnut Tree Farm* was reached.

Mr Leeds' grand house soon acquired the nickname *Mutton Hall* but did not stay isolated for very long as Shrub End Road became the victim of 1930s ribbon development. Mr Leeds played an active part in village life and provided the money for the annual Sunday School treat to Walton-on-the-Naze. As the coach left the church it would pull up outside *Mutton Hall* for the children to raise three cheers for Mr Leeds.

The improved living standards of the Shrub End inhabitants and developments of services provided by nearby Colchester led to a rash of development in the parish. By this time there was a regular bus service between the *Leather Bottle* and Colchester, and a water supply, along with other services, had reached the village. Colchester, like many other towns in the country was

Mutton Hall, Mr Leeds House, 45, Shrub End Rd.

c2000   *2023*

Geoff Pettit

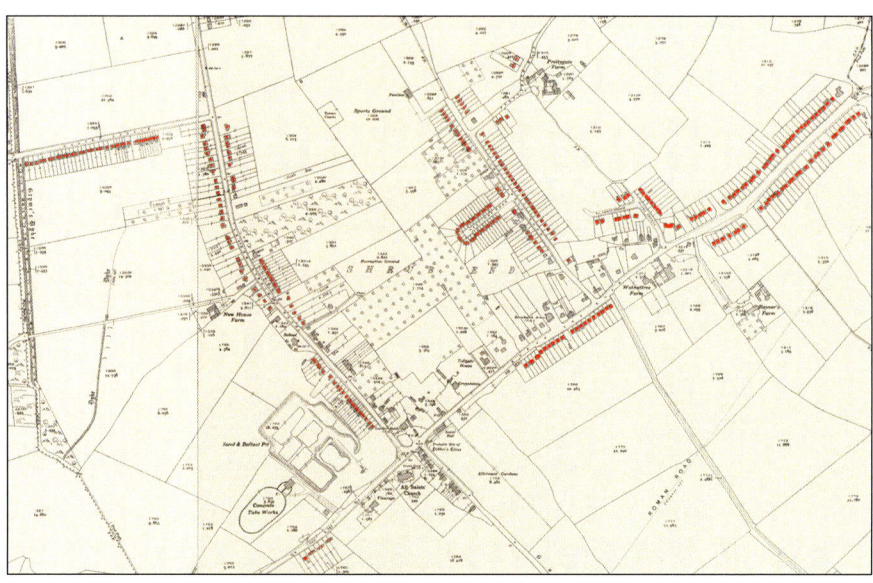

Extract from the 1939 OS 25 inch map with the 1930s houses highlighted in red.

expanding, and enterprising local builders could erect new houses wherever they chose. A popular choice was along roads that had accessible services. There were several such roads radiating from Colchester including Shrub End Road. This was called ribbon development and is well illustrated by what happened to Shrub End during this period. The longest roads in the parish, Shrub End Road, Straight Road, and King Harold Road were all lined with houses at this time. Most were detached or semidetached, many in the Tudorbethan style exhibiting fake beams and stained glass windows designed to appeal to the aspiring middle-class of the time.

Bernard Polley

King Harold Road. 1930s

King Harold Road. 2023

Although the majority of houses built at this time were ribbon developments there were a small number of new roads built. Within the parish the only example of this is Hastings Road. This is a cul-de-sac off King Harold Road and when initially built consisted of pairs of identical three bedroom semidetached units.

Hastings Road. 2023

300-310 Shrub End Road. 1930s

300-310 Shrub End Road. 2023

Bernard Polley

The first significant industrial activity in the parish occurred during this period. It was the opening of the gravel pit opposite the church, now Westlands Country Park. It would appear that a Mr Hutton, whilst on a trip to Australia, in 1925, saw sand and gravel being extracted commercially; when he returned home he acquired this site and set up in business, copying what he had seen in Australia.

Extract from the 1939 OS 25 inch map showing Mr Hutton's Sand & Ballast Pit.

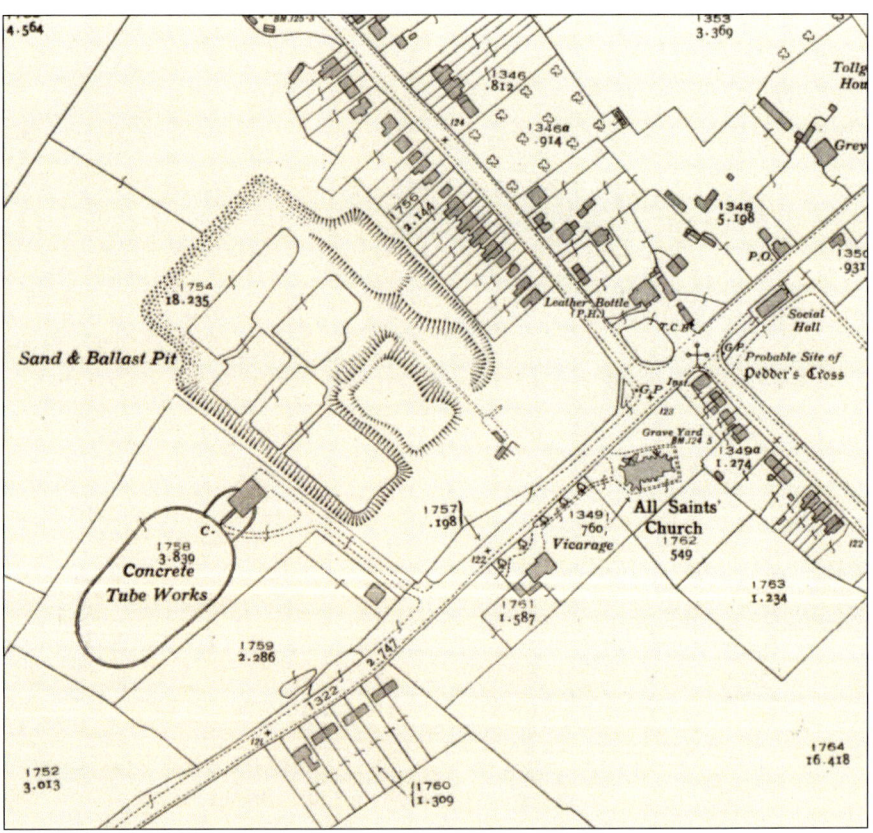

CHAPTER 6

WWII and the Post War Years

There is little remaining evidence of wartime activity within the parish but the consequence of the conflict and its aftermath has had a profound effect on the whole area.

I have seen the remains of a several WWII air raid shelters in nearby private gardens but am not aware of any within the parish. There is, however, one surviving shelter in public view in the playground of Straight Road School.

WWII air raid shelter for the children and staff of Straight Road School. 2022

Shrub End Road concrete road blocks.

There was another defensive structure built in the parish as a precaution in the event of a land invasion. This was an extension of Bluebottle Grove dyke that was dug as far as Shrub End Road. This road was equipped with concrete blocks, which could be used to control traffic and create a tank trap.

Post WWII there were major national reforms including a New Education Act, the Town & Country Planning Act, the creation of a National Health Service, in short everything needed to create a nation fit for heroes. All these reforms had their effect on the development of Shrub End.

The Town and Country Planning Act was designed to ensure that post-war building and development would be for the benefit of all by the democratisation of the use of land. This was to be achieved by giving local authorities wide-ranging powers. Each authority was required to produce a comprehensive development plan that included fulfilling the social, environmental and economic objectives of the area. Landowners could no longer change the use of land without the permission of the local authority who considered the impact of any development, large or small, on the whole area. In addition the local authorities were provided with financial support to carry out the redevelopment of land or to buy land and lease it to private developers.

Colchester Borough Council had acquired Walnut Tree Farm and Rayner's Farm in the 1930s but they had been unable to carry out whatever plans they had for it due to WWII. Post-war, new plans for a housing development were prepared. These included a variety of dwellings including flats, semidetached and terrace houses, and bungalows suitable for the elderly and infirm. The estate would also be provided with shops, places of worship, open spaces and schools.

Many residents moved into the new dwellings before the project was anywhere near complete. The Pettit family moved in 1951 and I reproduce here an extract from what one of them, Geoff, wrote in 1998. 'My parents received notification that their application for a council house was now successful and that No 6 Eldred Avenue, on the new Shrub End Estate, had been reserved for them and their five sons. We had, for the last 4 years, been living in a two-bedroomed house in West Stockwell Street, actually it only had one bedroom – the other was a very large landing. The house had been a 16th century public house called *The Victoria*, and after it had ceased trading in 1911 it was converted into two houses. There was no bathroom and the toilet was

Geoff Pettit

The building of Rayner Road on the former Rayner's farm in progress in 1951.

outside across the yard. On 21st March 1951 we moved into our luxurious four-bedroom house, that not only had an outside toilet, but an inside one along with a bath. There was an entrance hall, two living rooms and a kitchen, which included a coke boiler for hot water, a gas copper and a pantry. Outside there was a fair sized garden, about 120ft (36m) deep, there was a nice-sized brick-built shed, a coal shed, and a toilet, and to finish it of a small front garden.'

Many of the gardens of the council houses built

WWII poster to encourage people to grow their own food.

at this time had quite large gardens. The residents who moved into these houses who had stayed on home soil during the war had been encouraged to 'Dig for Victory' and many of them did. The philosophy of the Councils was to encourage them to continue growing their own food by providing them with large gardens. An allotment is traditionally measured in rods (perches or poles) (25 square metres), an old measurement dating back to Anglo-Saxon times. Ten rod is the accepted size of an allotment, an area equivalent to 250 square metres or about the size of a doubles tennis court. Some post WWII council houses were built with ten rod gardens, an area from which a reasonably competent gardener could feed a family of four.

To begin with, services to the estate were pretty minimal. The Coop sent a caravan twice a week until it opened its two shops in 1955. One was a butcher's and the other a grocer's, both situated in Iceni Square. They were soon joined by other shops, Hutt the Chemist, Chester the Newsagent, Sheppards Shoe Shop, Rothers General Store, a Hairdresser, and a Fish & Chip Shop.

Many of the families had children who were approaching school age and two schools were in the process of being built. On the eastern side of the estate there was King's Ford Junior and Infants School, which opened in January 1954 with 48 children. By Christmas that year it had risen to 327 in a school that was built for 240. At the western corner of the estate, on the site of the Shrub End wartime allotments, Gosbecks Primary School was built and opened in 1957. Many of the primary school children who entered this school had received their

Shrub End shops. 1976

Shrub End shops. 2022

infant education either in the Straight Road School, the Schoolroom in King Harold Road, or both.

Now we come to the secondary education facilities that were provided for children on the new estate.

During the early years of the 20th century most children attended an elementary school, which provided an education up to the age of 14. The changes in technology and emerging employment opportunities for

Leona Bryan

King's Ford Junior School. 1954. In 2015 the school became the Iceni Academy. 2023

Leona Bryan

Gosbecks Primary School opened 1957   *Gosbecks Primary School 2022*

women after WWI meant many more pupils wanted the opportunity to continue their education than there were facilities for them to do so.

To fulfill this demand many local Education Authorities, including Colchester, established selective Central Schools. These provided an improved general education of a practical character, sometimes with a slight industrial or commercial bias, for pupils between the ages of 11 and 15. The Central school in Colchester occupied part of the school premises at Hamilton Road and it was this school, established in 1920, that moved into the new Alderman Blaxill School premises on the Shrub End Estate in 1955.

As part of the school's Jubilee celebrations in 1980 the headmaster, W W Dent, recalled the move. 'At long last, in June 1955, the new buildings were ready, and I recall, as though it were yesterday, that walk to Shrub End, each pupil laden with text books and exercise books. But still more vividly do I remember the surprise, the wonder, and the delight expressed by face and voice as one amenity after another was discovered. Inside toilets! Showers! A gym! A playing field on site! A kitchen! A dining space! A medical room! How those children enjoyed and appreciated the good things they had never had before. And how well they treated them, and their new surroundings. Five years later, representatives from the building department at Chelmsford visited the school and expressed astonishment at the condition of fittings, paintwork, and furniture.'

The school continued to excel in Technical Studies, Home Economics, Drama, Business Studies, and before too long many of the teachers found they were teaching children's children. The changes in secondary education provision eventually led to the closure of the school in 2014.

The buildings were demolished in 2020 and the site is now occupied by two secondary education establishments, The Paxman Academy, which opened in 2022, and the North-East Essex Cooperative Academy that opened in 2023.

An early picture of Alderman Blaxill School.

Above: The Paxman Academy.   *Below: North-East Essex Cooperative Academy.*

The medical and spiritual wellbeing of the residents was taken care of at the purpose built Shrub End Surgery, now part of Colchester Medical Practice, and the new churches of St Cedd and of St John the Baptist.

St Cedd's is a sister church to All Saints' and was opened in 1955.

Shrub End Surgery, Shrub End Road. 2023

It was one of first dual-purpose churches to be built in this part of the country. The large hall is used for worship on Sundays and for a variety of social events on other days of the week. This was intended as a temporary arrangement but is still in existence serving the community in a wide variety of ways.

Close by St Cedd's is the Catholic Church of St John the Baptist. This is one of several chapels-of-ease to St James the Less, Colchester. It was built to serve the needs of those of Catholic faith who had moved to Shrub End. It opened in March 1961 with a seating capacity of 180. The building is a church hall-like structure, built of yellow stock brick laid in stretcher bond, with gable ends. The roadside end has a round arched entrance with a small arched window opening in the gable above: the other gable at the east end has two tall narrow lancet windows.

St Cedd's, Church of England. 2023

St John the Baptist, Catholic Church. 2023

Close by the newly built churches was another new building that provided the opportunities for people to get together and socialise. The *Ancient Briton* public house opened in 1956 and its outward appearence has changed little since.

The Ancient Briton. 2022

On a summer evening the forecourt is shaded by one of the old oak trees that survived the post war building. This tree, like several others of a similar size, on the estate is about 100 years old. There are a few even more ancient specimens that are estimated to be around 220 years old. These would have sprouted from acorns in the boundary hedges of the fields in Walnut Tree Farm and Rayner's Farm around 1800 and were recorded on the 1st edition of the 25 inch OS map. These trees are the oldest surviving reminders of the history of this area.

The 1870 OS map that shows field boundaries and trees superimposed upon a Shrub End Estate street map. Most of the surviving trees are highlighted in green. The age of an oak tree can be estimated by measuring its girth in centimetres, about a metre above ground level, and dividing by 2.5. Some of the Shrub End oaks are over 220 years old.

At the same time as the Shrub End Estate was being built, a similar development was taking place on the other side of Shrub End Road on the former lands of Prettygate Farm. A name that was soon adopted for the whole area even though building at this time went well beyond the extent of the lands belonging to this particular farm. Also, within the parish, building was taking place along Dugard Avenue and into Oaklands Estate.

Left: Semidetached houses in Prettygate Road built to a Bondrite design. Purchase price in 1957 was £1,350

Opposite:The Commons. 1969

Below: The Bondrite design showing its very efficient use of space.

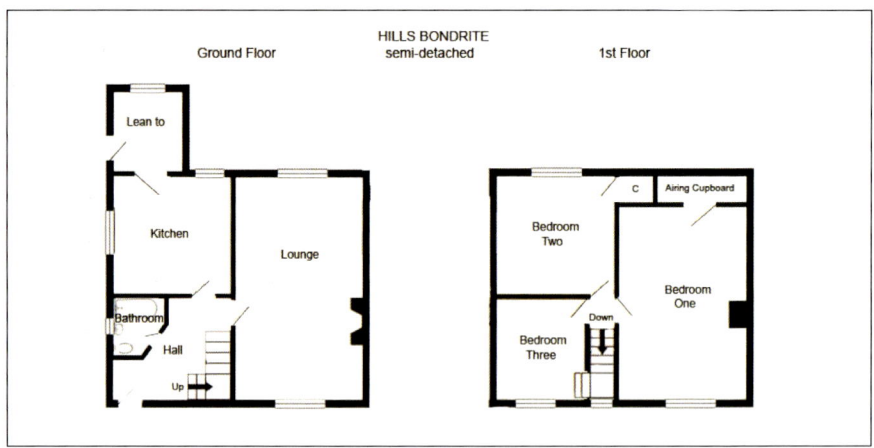

HILLS BONDRITE
semi-detached

Ground Floor

Lean to

Kitchen

Lounge

Bathroom

Hall

Up

1st Floor

C   Airing Cupboard

Bedroom Two

Bedroom One

Down

Bedroom Three

Bernard Polley

The Prettygate estate was a mixed council/private development of some 1750 units designed to provide accommodation for about 4000 individuals. It was a mixture of flats, houses and bungalows with most of the work carried out by the local builders, W A Hills & Sons Ltd. Many of the detached and semidetached houses were built to the open plan 'Bondrite' design. Some of the new properties were sold to individuals; some were purchased by industrial or commercial enterprises in the town for their employees, others reserved for council employees such as members of the police force and teaching profession, leaving many that were retained by the Council.

*Left: Handy Fisher Court.
Named after Handy H
Fisher Colchester Mayor
1938-9. Tallest building
at centre of Commons
view. 2023
Below: Two of the many
bungalows similar to one
in foreground of Commons
view. 2023*

*Below left: Houses being
built in Van Dyck Road.
1961
Below right: Occupied
houses in Van Dyck
Road. 1963*

The community was soon served by a selection of shops that opened in the block designed by Moyia Hills and built by W A Hills & Sons Ltd. This opened in 1959 and included two grocery stores, the Coop and International, next door was The Gaiety newsagents, followed by Morley chemists and Albany, dry cleaners. Above these retail outlets was a ladies hairdressing salon together with some residential flats. Across the road was a branch of Barclays Bank and Fisher's ironmongers store. A separate building housed a wool shop, a butchers and another hair salon.

Prettygate shops opened in 1959 as Albany, dry cleaners; Morley, chemists; Gaiety, newsagents; International Stores; Coop Store. Now All Care, community care services; Lloyds pharmacy; Cat Rescue, charity shop; Coop Funeral Services; Coop Store. 2023

Some years later in 1975, opposite the original W A Hills block the Prettygate branch library opened. This was built by Cadmans, and was accompanied by another four shops, Phase2 stationers, Woodlarks DIY shop, Lasts bakery and a laundrette.

Over the years the nature of these retail outlets have changed reflecting the changing demographic of the area. They now include The Coffee Hog café, Crazy Chef takeaway, All Care Mobility, and a Coop funeral parlour.

Next to the shops is the Prettygate Public House which opened in 1960 and for many years displayed the original ornamental gate that gave the area its name. The gate is now depicted in the carefully crafted three-dimensional pub sign.

Prettygate House plaque on the building housing the first of the Prettygate shops.
2022

Prettygate Library built and opened in 1975.
2022

The Prettygate. 2022

Prettygate Junior School opened in May 1959 in spacious surroundings. The buildings were designed with a corridor link between the teaching and administrative areas. The school has two libraries, assembly hall equipped with physical training facilities, classrooms, and a computer suite. The Infants School opened in 1962 and is situated behind the Junior School and shares the same grounds.

Secondary education was provided the Phillip Morant School & College adjacent to the Prettygate Estate but outside the ecclesiastical parish of Shrub End.

Next to the Prettygate school grounds was the Congregational Church that was built and opened in 1955. This was a replacement for the chapel in King Harold Road, which could no longer accommodate

Prettygate Schools. 2023

Prettygate Baptist Church. 2022

The old Plume Avenue United Reformed Church. c1980

Plume Avenue United Reformed Church. 2023

their growing congregation. The Prettygate schools experienced similar overcrowding as those on the Shrub End Estate but could, conveniently overflow into the weekday-empty neighbouring church building.

Plume Avenue Congregational church was not the only non-conformist sect to build a place of worship in the new Prettygate Estate. It was soon to be joined by Prettygate Baptist church.

This came about because a Trust Deed that belonged to a former Strict Baptist Church on St John's Green, Colchester became available. This church ceased in 1955 and was pulled down to make way for Colchester's southern relief road, Southway.

A group of eleven friends under the chairmanship of Pastor Martin of Zion Baptist, Ipswich worshipped in the King Harold Road chapel. Membership grew and by 1963 work had commenced on a purpose built chapel in Prettygate Road and the first service to be held in the new building took place in August 1967 with a newly appointed minister, Pastor Philip Grist. This first building was the present chapel hall. The new church building, attached to the hall was completed and opened in September 1976.

In 1972, Congregationalists merged with Presbyterians to form the United Reformed Church. By 1992 Plume Avenue church was too small, so £150,000 was raised to build new church complex, and in February 1993 the first service was held in the new sanctuary.

The King Harold Road chapel building was taken over by another religious sect and was called The Jesus Centre. It has since been renamed The Life House.

The Church of the Later Day Saints, Straight Road. 2022

That leaves The Church of Jesus Christ of Latter Day Saints. The Mormon Church in Straight Road was built between 1963 and 1965 mostly by members of the church at a cost of £65,000 supplied by the central body of Mormons. The church with its striking spire was designed by Graham & Baldwin of Stanford le Hope, Essex. The interior of the building has a sanctuary that is not unlike a non-conformist chapel.

As to the medical problems experienced by the expanding Prettygate population, these were looked after by the Ambrose Avenue Surgery. Dr Dennis Lamont opened this in 1958 in what was a private house, he was soon joined by Drs Chris Hall and Peter Snell. It is now operated as a Group Practice with ten General Practitioners and its own pharmacy.

The Ambrose Avenue Surgery. 2023

All the building and associated activities during the postwar period kept people busy and just about every aspect of life was improving, but underneath this newfound peace there was, simmering beneath the surface, the Cold War. This was the state of military tension and potential hostility between the American and Soviet power blocks. Both were in possession of nuclear weapons with the potential for mutual assured destruction (MAD). To help mitigate this potential catastrophe and/or prepare for the aftermath several early warning and monitoring systems were established in the UK. One of these was the establishment of a network of observation stations.

These were manned by the Royal Observer Corps (ROC) which was formed in 1925 and became the 'eyes and ears' of the Royal Air Force. Then during the Cold War, 1955-1991, civilian volunteers were trained and administered by professional full-time officers to man the 1560 bunkers established all over the UK.

One of the Essex ROC Group HQs was based in Lexden Road, Colchester and one of its bunkers was located in the parish of Shrub End near the top of Olivers Lane, now the cul-de-sac Gosbecks View. I remember this as a low concrete structure housing a manhole cover not dissimilar to many other manhole covers that provide access to underground services.

I did not know at the time that this was the access shaft to a ROC bunker. Each of these was constructed of reinforced concrete 15ft (4.5 m) below ground level and consisted of a main room 15ft x 7ft (4.5m x 2.1m) with two smaller rooms. The main room housed the monitoring and communication equipment, bunk beds, and survival necessities. The only other communication to the surface was a ventilation shaft and a tube used for radiation detectors.

The ROC volunteers carried out regular exercises involving visits of various durations to maintain their preparedness in the event of disaster. By 1968, due to advances in technology the Government decided that radiation monitoring could be done remotely and the network of bunkers was no longer necessary.

A few of the 67 Essex bunkers have survived and are open to the public, others still exist in various states of preservation and are visited by enthusiasts and urban explorers but there are many that have compltely dissapeared leaving no visible trace at all.

The Olivers Lane installation falls into the last category although on this site there are no visible remains, a mysteriously well-protected undisturbed patch of grass exists surrounded by more recent developments.

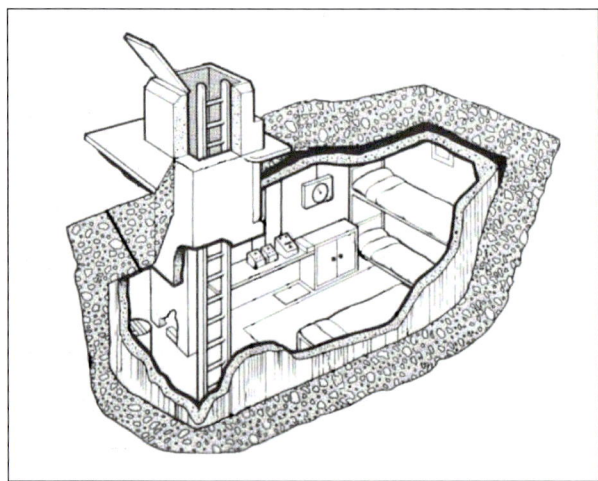

Left: A cut-away sketch of the type of ROC bunker installed in Shrub End.

Below: The Site of the Shrub End bunker today where there are no visible remains. 2023

After the initial surge of post war development during the 1950s and 60s building slowed somewhat and the only sizable area lost to agricultural use during the 1970s was that now occupied by Westlands estate. This can be accessed only from Straight Road and fills the whole area between this road and Stanway Green, Dugard Avenue and Westlands Country Park.

A further green area that was not developed until the 1980s was the Coop playing field off King Harold Road. This former large open space is now occupied by houses accessed from an extended Scythe Way and a new cul-de-sac named Regency Green for reasons I have been unable to determine.

Then just before the end of the century the creation of Colchester Archaeological Park led to the first sizable housing development to the south of Gosbecks Road. This, the Roman Fields estate, consists of detached houses accompanied by a small number of affordable terrace and semidetached dwellings The whole estate is accessed by way of a maze of cul-de-sacs named after something vaguely Roman.

The area of land to the east of Layer Road that was not moved into the parish until 1960 was home to a selection of army properties. The oldest of these were built as married quarters immediately after WWII when there was a great shortage of building materials and skilled labour. This situation led to the rise of the factory-made prefabricated houses. The style chosen by the military were those manufactured by Airey. This design was developed by Leeds based builder Sir Edwin Airey in 1947. The design used the minimum of imported materials and could be erected with little equipment using unskilled labour. The house kits could be provided for a variety of house sizes and layouts. The most common option was the three-bedroom semi and this was the style chosen for the army estate. Airey houses used steel and concrete frames clad with overlapping pre-cast concrete slabs, a technology first developed

A pair of Airey three-bedroom semis.

by the firm in the early 1920s and perfected in the successful 1947 design, which resulted in the nationwide building of 26,000 Airey houses during the ten years following 1945.

By 1955 the building industry had caught up and firms like W H Hills could build their Bondrite houses using conventional techniques as an economical option (page 192).

The Airy houses in Shrub End were refurbished and clad in brick in the late 20th century.

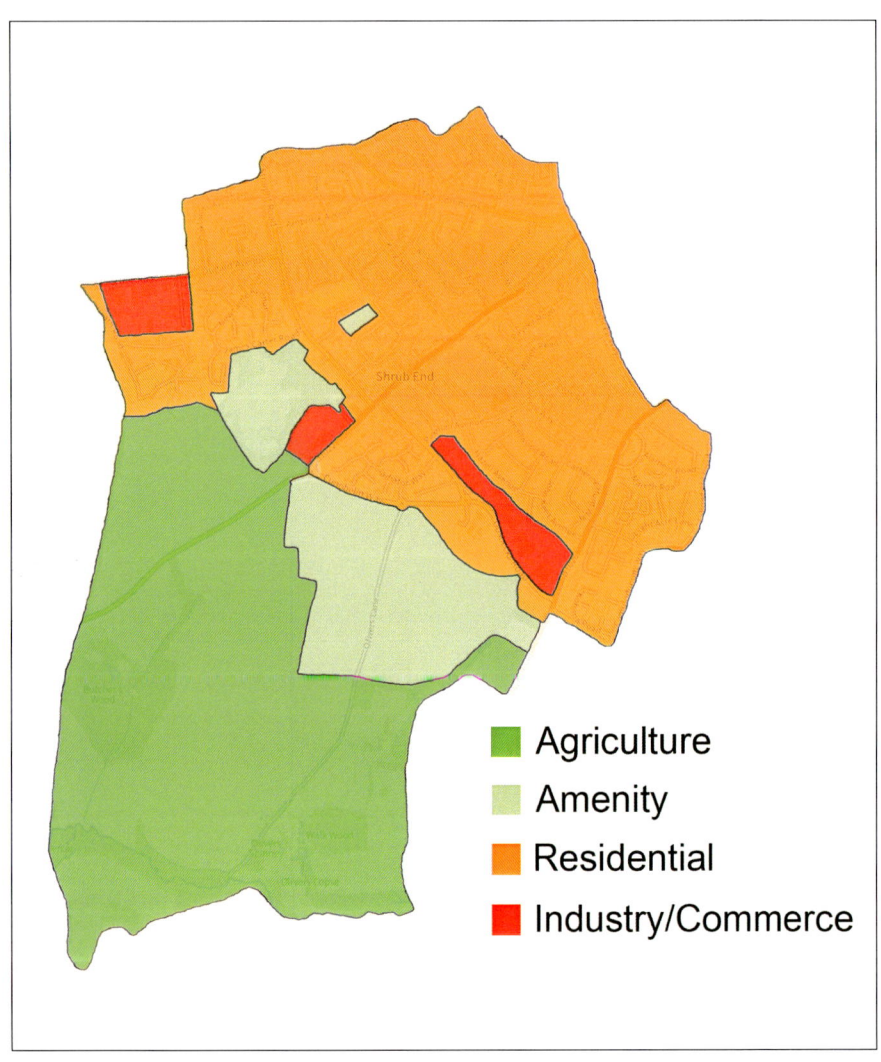

For most of its history the majority of the land in the parish of Shrub End was in agricultural use. By the 21st century approximately half was occupied by commercial and residential developments

CHAPTER 7

The 21st century

There have not been any significant changes to the use of the land in the parish of Shrub End during the first quarter of the 21st century. There has however been considerable rebuilding and continued minor infilling and back-land developments.

During the early years of the century the Ministry of Defence sold off many of their older properties, including some of those within the parish. Some were bought by individuals, others by developers who

Fortuna Park, a mixed housing development. 2023

proceeded to fill in the open spaces. One of the largest of these was Fortuna Park. This is a mixed development of houses, apartments and social housing that was completed by 2010.

A smaller development occurred in King Harold Road in 2016 when Godwin Close with its five bungalows replaced number 91 in its large garden.

The most noticeable changes that have taken place this century have been those within the principal zones of industrial and commercial activity. These are concentrated in three areas. The first of these is along part of Shrub End Road on land that was formerly part of Brickwall Farm. The second occupies nearly a half of land of the former New House Farm, and the third sits on the land of Gosbecks Farm and Lambert's Farm situated on the north side of Gosbecks Road.

Colchester City Civic Amenity Recycling Centre with
the now well established Westlands Country Park in the background.

The oldest industrial area of any size in the parish was the gravel pit opened by Mr Hutton in 1925 (described on p180). This was later sold to Hoveringham Gravels Ltd and then in 1959 it was taken over by Essex County Council who continued to extract gravel but also used it as a landfill site. Gravel extraction ceased in 1975 and the landfill site was closed in 1990. The site was then capped with clay and landscaped to be leased to Colchester Borough Council who, in 2007 opened it to the public as the now established Westlands Country Park. There remains a relatively small area that is now used as a Civic Amenity Recycling Centre for the City of Colchester along with a few industrial/commercial units along Shrub End Road.

Mansell's Bonded Fabrics occupied one of the largest of these until the disastrous fire on the 18ᵗʰ December 1992 that totally destroyed

Aerial view of Mansell's factory with Lay & Wheeler's warehouse in the foreground and the Leather Bottle beyond. 1984

Bernard Polley

Bernard Polley

Aerial view of Mansell's factory on fire. 1992

the factory. Mansell's site was later developed as a residential complex aptly named Phoenix Court.

Close by is the short cul-de-sac, Pedders Close, which provides access to the former Lay & Wheeler warehouse that is now occupied by AM Logistics & Warehousing. Also in Pedders Close are premises currently used by Elfin Kitchens, manufacturers of mini kitchens, and Chaffy Ltd who offer corporate entertainment and hospitality services.

Beyond Pedders Close is a considerable area occupied by AK Metals Recycling. In front of this stands the oldest building on this site, the bungalow that originally stood at the entrance to Mr Hutton's gravel

Phoenix Court. 2023

pit and which for over forty years was occupied by Mankim Models. This business closed in 2018 and the premises are now occupied by Tolly Paving and Detect2, a company offering computer and media services.

Next is the largest building on this site, the purpose built self-storage facility operated by StorageMart. Then between this and the entrance to Colchester's Recycling Centre are two automotive companies, Abbey Motors and Colchester Tyres.

The second of our industrial/commercial zones is in Peartree Road. Various branches of the firm of Cadman occupy a good proportion of

213 Shrub End Road, Mankim Models. 2018

213 Shrub End Road, Tolly Paving and Detect2. 2022

In 2016 StorageMart opened. 2023

this site. This business was started by two brothers who, with the help of their father, in 1932 operated as general builders. The firm was successful which led to rapid expansion during the 1960s and 70s and now operates as the C M Cadman Group Ltd from Cadman House, Maurice Way.

Another firm with a long association with the local area is Hatfields. This was established by John Hatfield in 1886 in the front room of his house in St John's Street, Colchester. The expanding home furnishing business moved to a purpose-built new store in Peartree Road in 1975.

The rest of the Peartree Road site is occupied by over 30 units of a range of sizes occupied by an ever-changing variety of companies and organisations offering a wide spectrum of products and services.

Hatfields' first out of town store. 1975

The refronted Hatfields. 2023

Moving on to Gosbecks Road, the location of the third industrial and commercial zone in the parish. One of the first commercial buildings on this site was at the Layer Road end where Kent Blaxill erected a purpose-built facility for their business. This had been founded as an oil and colour business in Colchester High Street by John Kent in 1838. He went on to form a partnership with Edwin Blaxill in 1867 and this expanded and diversified into a flourishing supplier of building materials. The managing director of the business for the years 1935-1952 was Alec E Blaxill. He was also an Alderman and Mayor of Colchester in 1909-10 and 1937-38. Kent Blaxill was a major supplier of paint, timber, glass, ironmongery and much more when they moved into their new premises on the corner of Layer Road and Gosbecks Road in 1966. At this time out-of-town shopping was a pioneering idea.

Aerial view of the first 'out of town' Kent Blaxill premises. 1966

Leona Bryan

Leona Bryan

Above: Granville Garages. 1963

Left: Before self-service the customer asked a petrol pump attendant, here David H King, for the desired number of gallons and paid him with cash.

Below: Granville Garages, now Roy Tolley premises. 2023

At the other end of the Gosbecks Road commercial zone was Granville Garage. It was owned by Mr S M G Hall who had opened a garage in Military Road opposite Granville Road. After which he named his garage and kept when he moved to new premises in Gosbecks Road. During the early 1970s it was taken over by Roy Tolley who had moved out of town from his Butt Road premises. This proved to be a good move for the business as it had the space to flourish into the family-owned garage and major dealership it is today.

The intervening spaces were gradually occupied by a variety of factories and organisations. One that survives from the early days is Alstons, the furniture manufacturer. This firm was started in 1860 by two brothers William and Ambrose Alston who opened a furniture shop in Sudbury. This outgrew its premises in the town and moved Colchester where they occupied several sites before settling in Gosbecks Road in 1964. Here they continue to operate as a successful manufacturer and supplier of well-engineered soft furnishings.

Another site formerly occupied by the Wheeler family who owned Colchester Wine Company, is now occupied by a Lidl Supermarket that opened in 2016.

For many years Colchester Council owned a considerable area of this zone which was used by the Works Department and as a base for Colchester Borough Homes. Most of this has now been sold. Other premises in the zone are currently occupied by a range of manufacturers, wholesalers, and retailers.

Above: Alstons. 1964
Below: Alstons 2023

In the 21st century ecclesiastical boundaries have little relevance to the majority of the population. Nevertheless the ecclesiastical parish of Shrub End has been a convenient demarcation for the area of land that is the subject of this book. For most of the last two-thousand years or so the majority of the land use has been agricultural. Then during the last hundred years or thereabouts

Lidl supermarket. 2023

this has been eaten into by residential, commercial, industrial, and leisure developments, which now occupy about half the land area of the parish.

This means that now all the necessities for the provision of a reasonable 21ˢᵗ century lifestyle are available within the parish for those who choose to use them.

As well as generally good quality housing, adequate educational and recreational facilities there is a range of wholesale and retail outlets including, specialist and general shops and a supermarket all within a mile or two of each other. All this as well as easy access to the countryside makes Shrub End a desirable place to live. Of course not all types of employment opportunities are available within the parish but there are excellent transport links into the City of Colchester and further afield where most can be found within an hours travel time.

With the increased opportunities for working from home it is possible that an increasing number of residents will need to leave the parish less often. The resulting reduction of vehicle use and possible increase in walking and cycling between local destinations may make the parish an even more desirable area in which to live.

My hope is that this book has opened the eyes of readers to what they may not have noticed is on their doorstep, to appreciate it, and to look after it for future generations.

APPENDIX

The Parish of Shrub End Street Names

Army:	*army and former army lands east of Layer Road*
Gosbecks Fm	*development around Gosbecks Farm*
Roman Fields	*development off Gosbecks Road*
Orchard	*development between King Harold Rd and Straight Rd*
Prettygate	*Prettygate area*
Shrub End	*Shrub End estate*
Stanway Grn	*Stanway Green area*
Westlands	*estate to the west of Straight Road*

Alamein Road	Army	Commemorates the WWII battles in Egypt.
Alan Way	Prettygate	The Christian name of one of the members of the Hills Family, who developed the estate.
All Saints Avenue	Prettygate	After the parish of All Saints, Shrub End.
Ambrose Avenue	Prettygate	From the Christian name of one of the developers, William Ambrose Hill.
Araken Close	Army	Arakan is a coastal region in South-east Asia.
Aurora Drive	Gosbecks Fm	The Roman goddess of dawn.
Baden Powell Drive	Orchard	This with other roads on the Orchard Estate in Shrub End was named to commemorate the centenary year of the Boy Scout Movement.
Bale Close	Westlands	After Major John Edward Bale, 1833-1913. A Colchester, architect and a prolific artist.

Barbour Gardens	Roman Fields	Named after the family who owned Gosbecks Farm before the Archaeological Park.
Becker Road	Westlands	After Harry Becker, 1865-1928, a Suffolk painter and lithographer.
Bellona Way	Gosbecks Fm	Ancient Roman goddess of war.
Bishop Road	Shrub End	Named after Major John Bishop, who was Mayor seven times between 1863 and 1876.
Boadicea Way	Shrub End	Named for Boadicea or Boudicca, Queen of the Iceni.
Breachfield Road	Army	A field name in this area.
Brownsea Close	Orchard	To commemorate the centenary of the Scout Association,named after Brownsea Island where the first Scout camp was held in 1907.
Camulodunum Way	Army	An ancient Celtic name derived from the home of Camulos, the god of war.
Camulus Close	Roman Fields	After the Celtic god of war
Cape Close	Prettygate	After H.J. Cape, headmaster of the Grammar School 1916-37.
Cassino Road	Army	The Battles of Cassino, Italy saw fierce fighting during 1944.
Catherine Hunt Way	Shrub End	Named after Dame Katherine Hunt, Mayor in 1924 and the the first woman Alderman for the Borough.

Centurian Way	Roman Fields	After the Roman connection with the site.
Cherrywood Drive	Prettygate	Named after the very many cherry trees that grew in the area
Clara Reeve Close	Westlands	Clara Reeve 1729-1807 was an Ipswich born author who lived in Colchester for some years.
Cohort Drive	Roman Fields	After the Roman connection with the site.
Commons	Prettygate	see: The Commons
Coriolanus Close	Roman Fields	After the Roman general Gaius Marcius Coriolanus.
Crome Close	Prettygate	After John Crome, an English landscape painter.
Cunobelin Way	Roman Fields	Cunobelin, Shakespeare's Cymbeline was King of the Britons during the 1st century.
Corunna Drive	Army	Named for the Battle of Corunna in 1809, during the Napoleonic Wars.
Daniell Drive	Shrub End	After a very old Colchester family. Jeremiah Daniell was Mayor in 1720, 1725 and 1740.
Devon Road	Shrub End	Built at the time of the war in Korea (1950's), and named after the Devonshire Regiment.
Dugard Avenue		Formerly Peartree Road or Lane, after William Dugard, Headmaster of the Royal Grammar School from 1637-1642/3.

Duncan Road	Shrub End	For Dr. Peter Martin Duncan, a physician at Colchester Hospital and a great antiquarian. He discovered the fallen Roman Gate at the north-east corner of Holly Trees Meadow, now known as the Duncan Gate. He was Mayor in 1857.
Egerton-Green Road	Shrub End	After members of the Egerton-Green family.
Eldred Avenue	Shrub End	The Eldreds were Lords of the Manor of Oliver's from Queen Elizabeth's reign.
Elmwood Avenue	Army	A field name in this area.
Fenno Close	Westlands	From old Norse *Finnr* meaning person from Finland.
Gainsborough Rd	Prettygate	After the landscape and portrait artist Thomas Gainsborough 1727-88, born in Sudbury.
Gilwell Park Close	Orchard	To commemorate the centenary of the Scout Association.
Gladiator Way	Roman Fields	Named after Roman Gladiators who fought in amphitheatres.
Glebe Road	Army	A field name in this area.
Glisson Square	Shrub End	After Dr. Francis Glisson 1597-1677, Regius Professor of Physics at Cambridge from 1637 until his death. He came to live in St.Mary's Parish in 1640 and practised there.

Gloucester Avenue   Shrub End   Built at the time of the Korean War this road commemorates the Gloucester Regiment.

Godwin Close   off King Harold Rd   Godwin was the father of King Harold.

Gosbecks Road   From Gosbecks Farm.

Gosbecks View   Gosbecks Rd   Named after nearby Gosbecks Roman site.

Greystones Close off Shrub End Rd   Built in the grounds of the house called Greystones.

Grymes Dyke Way   Stanway Green After the ancient earthwork.

Gurney Benham Close Shrub End   After Sir Gurney Benham, Alderman and Mayor in 1892, 1908 and 1933. He was High Steward and an Honorary Freeman. Sir Gurney Benham was a local historian. For many years he was editor of the Essex County Standard, owned by Benham Newspapers.

Harvey Road   Shrub End   John Bawtree Harvey was Mayor in 1881, 1882 and 1884. Also commemorates Daniel Whittle Harvey M.P. for Colchester1818, 1820, 1831,1832.

Hastings Road   off King Harold Rd   Named by the developer after the Battle of Hastings.

Hazell Avenue   Shrub End   After George W. B. Hazell, Mayor in 1931. He was Chairman of the Housing Committee under the Housing Act 1936.

Heath Road	Stanway Grn	Stanway Heath was here. There was also a farm called Heath Farm.
Hedge Drive	Shrub End	Named after Thomas Hedge, Mayor 1787, 1801, 1804 and 1808 and Thomas Hedge Jnr. Mayor, 1807. Members of the Colchester clockmaking family.
Hills Crescent	Prettygate	From the developers S.W. Hills and W.A. Hills.
Hitherwood Road	Army	Hitherwood, field name in area.
Hoe Drive	Prettygate	After the farming implements used to make up Prettygate Farm gate.
Holman Crescent	Prettygate	After Rev. William Holman who spent many years collecting materials relating to the antiquities of Essex.
Holly Close	Army	MOD named many Closes after trees.
Homefield Road	Army	A field name in this area.
Iceni Way	Shrub End	The Iceni tribe was based in Norfolk and the northern half of Suffolk. Their leader was Queen Boadicea (Boudicca) who took revenge upon the Roman conquerors.
Imphal Close	Army	The Battle of Imphal took place in Manipur region of India in1944.
James Carter Road	Westlands	Local 19th century author of 'Essays on Taste' and 'Memoirs of a Working Man'

Jeffrey Close	Prettygate	After P. Shaw Jeffrey, headmaster of the Royal Grammar School 1900-16.
John Kent Avenue	Shrub End	After John Kent, mayor in 1879. Founder of Kent, Blaxill and Co. Ltd.
King Harold Road		After King Harold the Saxon King who was Lord of the Manor of Stanway, which at that time included part of Shrub End.
Knightsbridge Close	Army	Knightsbridge in central London
Kohima Road	Army	Battle of Kohima, 1944.
Landseer Road	Prettygate	After the artist Sir Edward Landseer 1802-73, a famous animal painter.
Laxton Court	Prettygate	Not known
Lordswood Road	Army	A field name in this area.
Mareth Road	Army	Commemorating the Battle of the Mareth line, March 1943.
Mason Close	Shrub End	Bernard Mason, Freeman of the Borough, local historian and authority on Colchester clockmakers. Mr Mason restored Tymperleys, the home of William Gilberd and gave it to the Borough together with his collection of Colchester made clocks.
Mercury Close	Roman Fields	Named after the Roman god Mercury who may have been worshipped at Gosbecks.

Moss Road	off Peartree Rd	Runs beside Gryme's Dyke. The middle English version of the biblical name 'Moses'.
Munnings Road	Prettygate	After the artist Sir Alfred Munnings 1878-1959, born in Suffolk and lived at Dedham. He specialised in painting horses.
Nash Close	Prettygate	After the artist John Nash, R.A. (1893-1977) who lived at Wormingford.
Newcastle Avenue	Westlands	The most populous city in North-east England.
Norman Way	Prettygate	Presumably so named because of Colchester's Norman connections.
Oaklands Avenue	off Dugard Ave	Named after the large number of oak trees in this area.
Owen Ward Close	Shrub End	After A Owen Ward, Mayor of Colchester 1919
Parr Drive		D. Samuel Parr was a master of the Colchester Grammar School (1776-8), a voluminous writer.
Paxman Avenue	Shrub End	After James Paxman, Mayor 1887 and 1897. He founded of the firm of Davey Paxman & Co. Ltd.
Peartree Road		Continuation of Dugard Ave.
Pedders Close		Close to the supposed site of Pedder's Cross.
Pilborough Way	Westlands	After John Pilborough, printer and publisher of the *Colchester Journal* 1733-47.

Plough Drive	Prettygate	After the farming implements used to make up Prettygate Farm gate.
Plume Avenue	Prettygate	After Plume Farm, named after the family who owned it 1715-1845.
Prettygate Road	Prettygate	From the farm that took its name from its gate, which was made of agricultural implements.
Rangoon Close	Army	The largest city of Myanmar.
Rayner Road	Shrub End	Named after nearby Rayner's Farm.
Reaper Road	Prettygate	After the farming implements used to make up Prettygate Farm gate.
Red Mill		A 20th century development built on the site of a windmill 1820-1870.
Regency Green	off King Harold Rd	A Tarmac development of 1989. Name is the developer's choice.
Rembrant Way	Prettygate	After the Dutch painter Rembrandt van Rijn 1608-89.
Rimini Close	Army	The Battle of Rimini took place in 1944, one of the hardest battles fought by the Eighth Army.
Rowallen Close	Orchard	To commemorate the centenary of the Boy Scout Association. Lord Rowallan was the Chief Scout.
Rudsdale Way	Prettygate	After E.J. Rudsdale who was for many years connected with the Colchester and East Essex Museum.
Rutland Avenue	Shrub End	Was for many years England's smallest county.
Salamanca Way	Army	Commemorates the 1812 Battle of Salamanca, where the French forces were defeated by Wellington.

Salerno Crescent	Army	Commemorating Battle of Salerno, fought in Italy, in 1943.
Salmon Close	Westlands	From Latin *salmo*, possibly from *salire*-to leap.
Saxon Close	Prettygate	To commemorate the East Saxons after who Essex takes its name.
Scythe Way	Prettygate	After the farming implements used to make up Prettygate Farm gate.
Shilleto Close	Westlands	The surname was first recorded in Staffordshire where the family are believed to have descended ancient Saxon chieftain named *Scealda*.
Shrub End Road		Leads to Shrub End (the end of the heath or shrub).
Sittang Close	Army	Commemorating the Battle of Sittang Bridge 1942, part of the Burma campaign.
Somers Road	Orchard	To commemorate the centenary of the Scout Association. Lord Somers was a former Chief Scout.
Somerset Close	Shrub End	County of south-west England.
Sparling Close	Shrub End	After William Sparling, Mayor in 1805, 1813, 1828 and 1831.
Springfields Drive	Roman Fields	The surname is first recorded in Suffolk, as Lords of the manor of Lavenham. The family were important merchants in the cloth trade during the Middle Ages.
Stanfield Close	Stanway Grn	Possibly a field mane.
Straight Road		Because for about 2km of its length it is quite straight.

Sutton Park Avenue	Orchard	To commemorate the centenary of the Boy Scout Association. Sutton Park was a venue for several World Scout Jamborees.
Talavera Crescent	Army	Commemorating the 1809 Battle of Talavera, Sir Arthur Wellesley was enobled Viscount Wellington after the battle was won.
Temple Road	Roman Fields	After the Romano-British Temple on land formerly owned by Gosbecks Farm.
The Commons	Prettygate	This road skirts the old Common fields of the Borough.
Thracian Close	Roman Fields	After the Roman connection with the nearby Romano-British temple.
Toga Close	Roman Fields	Names in this area have a connection with the nearby Romano-British site.
Tumulus way	Roman Fields	Names in this area have a connection with the nearby Romano-British site.
Twining Road	Westlands	Growing or moving in a way that wraps around an object several times.
Valley Close	Stanway Grn	Named after a landscape feature.
Van Dyck Road	Prettygate	After the Flemish artist Sir Anthony Van Dyck 1559-1641.
Venus Road	Gosbecks Fm	Roman goddess of love
Veritas Grove	Gosbecks Fm	Roman goddess of truth
Vesta Lane	Gosbecks Fm	Roman goddess of hearth, home and family.
Victoria Mews	Army	After Queen Victoria

Wallis Court	Westlands	After Joseph Wallis, an ironmonger and ironfounder of Colchester.
Walnut Tree Way	Shrub End	Named after Walnut Tree Farm that was near here.
Watts Road	Shrub End	After Alderman Lent John Watts, Mayor of Colchester 1890-91.
Weavers Close	Prettygate	Named in commemoration of the Flemish refugee weavers of the 16th and 17th centuries, who settled in Colchester.
Wilkin Court	off King Harold Rd	After Frank Wilkin, Mayor of Colchester 1980-81.
Wilbye Close	Shrub End	After John Wilbye 1574-1638, the Elizabethan madrigal composer.
Willett Road	Shrub End	After William Willett 1856-1915, the originator of 'British Summer Time'. He spent much of his boyhood in Colchester.
Winston Avenue	Prettygate	In honour of Sir Winston Churchill 1874-1965. One of the most prominent figures of the 20th century political stage.
Wolton Road	Shrub End	Named after Henry Wolton, six times Mayor of Colchester between 1844 and 1861.
Worthington Way	Prettygate	From one of the Christian names of the developer, Stanley Worthington Hills.

Sellect Bibliography

Benham, Hervey   *Some Essex Watermills*
                                  1976   Essex County Newspapers Ltd
Benham's Directories   *Colchester*

Blaxill, Edwin Alec   *Lion Walk Congregational Church 1642-1937*
                                  1938   Benham & Co. Ltd
Edwards, Christina   *Parish of Stanway c1700-c1840*
                                  2001   Bellus Books
Edwards, Christina   *Parish of Stanway c1900-c1920*
                                  2010   Bellus Books
Crummy, Philip   *City of Victory*
                                  1997   Colchester Archaeological Trust
Elrington, C R (Editor)   *Victoria History of Essex IX*
                                  1994   OUP
Farries, Kenneth G   *Essex Windmills, Millers & Millwrights III*
                                  1984   Charles Skilton Ltd
Goulding, Charles (Editor)   *Historic Shrub End*
                                  1976   All Saints with St Cedd's
Grist, Philip A   *25 Years On, Prettygate Baptist Church*
                                  1986   Prettygate Baptist Church
Hazzel, Pauline   *The Journey to Shrub End*
                                  2015   Essex Bookbinders Ltd

Jephcott Jess A — *The Inns, Taverns and Pubs of Colchester*
1995   private publication
Kelly's Directories — *Colchester*

Morant, Philip — *History of Colchester 1st ed 1748*
1970   Phillimore
Pettit, Geoff — *Shrub End's Past in Old Photographs*
1990   All Saints with St Cedd's
Pettit, Geoff & Cooper, Richard — *Shrub End Looking Back*
1998   All Saints with St Cedd's
Polley, Bernard — *Prettygate*
2002   private publication
Polley, Bernard — *Pictorial Shrub End*
2004   private publication
Rickwood, Ken — *Colchester's Secret Roman River*
2019   David Cleveland
Stephenson, David — *The Book of Colchester*
1978   Barracuda Books Ltd
White, William — *History, Gazetteer & Directory of Essex*
1848   Robert Leader
Wright Thomas — *The History and Topography of Essex*
1836   George Virtue

INDEX

Figures in **bold** refer to illustrations

A

B

G

H

T

U

V

WXYZ